# *Keeping America's Promise to North Carolina's Children*

*a collection of true stories about children and youth in the 1990's*

**edited by Jennifer Toth**

*a publication of the*
North Carolina Child Advocacy Institute
*and*
Communities in Schools of North Carolina

To obtain additional copies of this publication, call 919-834-6623 or write NC Child Advocacy Institute, Attn: *America's Promise*, 311 East Edenton Street, Raleigh, NC 27601-1017.

Cover and text design by Carol Majors, Publications Unltd.

ISBN #  0-9665180-1-2

North Carolina Child Advocacy Institute
311 East Edenton Street, Raleigh, NC 27601-1017
919-834-6623 • www.ncchild.org

Communities in Schools of North Carolina
222 North Person Street
Raleigh, NC 27601
919-832-2700 • www.cisnc.org

# Acknowledgments

This collection of true stories is the realization of talent, enthusiasm and just plain hard work on the part of many people.

Our most heartfelt gratitude goes to the boys, girls and teenagers who populate these pages and teach us valuable lessons about ourselves, our communities and our state. Next, we thank and applaud the contributors — a mix of professional writers, journalists, and parents moved to share their personal stories. They always kept the best interests of children at heart and we celebrate their achievement with the publication of *Keeping America's Promise to North Carolina's Children*.

Our editor, Jennifer Toth, is deserving of particular gratitude. She guided these stories to a coherent whole while remaining sensitive to the children and youth, respectful of the writers and flexible with the process. We thank her for her keen insight.

We value our association with Communities in Schools of NC, the managing partner for America's Promise in the

Tarheel State. In particular, Linda Harrill and Laura Killion merit praise for their interest, their good work across our state and their efforts to ensure these stories are actually read, as well as written.

Several NC Child Advocacy Institute staff members have been involved from concept to completion. This volume simply would not exist were it not for the perseverance, talent and attention to detail evidenced by Sharon Reuss, who coordinated the whole effort. Jonathan Sher had the original idea of producing an anthology about "invisible" children in North Carolina—an idea that evolved into *Keeping America's Promise*; Helene Delgado, Annette Plummer and Stacy Smith offered valuable suggestions and encouragement; Barbara Robinson pitched in with administrative support; and Judy Auman, Katherine Kantner and Paula Wolf proofread with precision. We also acknowledge the sound advice of members of the Institute's Board of Directors and Council of Advisors.

Lastly, we appreciate the graphic design and book-building expertise provided by Carol Majors and Ann Farmer at Publications Unltd. ☜

Although a significant investment in this book was made both by the North Carolina Child Advocacy Institute and Communities in Schools of North Carolina, its development and production could not have been accomplished without external support. We are grateful for the financial assistance provided by the Smith Richardson Foundation, the A.J. Fletcher Foundation and the NC Department of Health and Human Services (Division of Social Services). Although these organizations have responsibility neither for any errors nor for the opinions expressed in this volume, we hope they share our sense of pride in this publication.

# Introduction

The North Carolina Child Advocacy Institute (NCCAI) and Communities in Schools of North Carolina (CISNC) work toward advancing the best interests of our state's children. Our two nonprofit, state-level organizations are located in Raleigh and often advise state officials. However, we're keenly aware that much of what affects kids isn't determined by state government or agencies... **but rather within local communities and neighborhoods across North Carolina**. *Keeping America's Promise to North Carolina's Children* provides you the opportunity to connect vivid illustrations of children and youth—their aspirations, their wants, their needs—with concrete examples of how you might serve in your community.

As collaborative partners in *Keeping America's Promise to North Carolina's Children*, we're delighted with what the authors have achieved in this anthology—this sampler—of real life stories. This book celebrates North Carolina children and youth who are remarkable in their diversity. Some dream and aspire to great heights, although they may seem invisible due to geography, ethnicity or culture. Others grow up fulfilled and happy, although they daily live with extraordinary challenges. This volume also applauds all the individual adults and organizations making, and keeping, the Promises that count to NC's children and youth.

NCCAI decided on the strategy of recruiting people *outside* the Raleigh Beltline to write feature stories about young North Carolinians and the adults who care enough about them to make them a genuine priority. CISNC (NC's managing partner for the America's Promise initiative) then solidified the thematic framework necessary to connect all these seemingly unrelated narratives.

Our call for submission of stories was directed to hundreds of editors, publishers and reporters across the state, Covenant with North Carolina's Children members, Communities in Schools affiliates, the NC Writers Network, NC Scholastic Media Association, NC Cooperative Extension Service and outreach through the religious community. We were seeking 20 to 25 stories. Little did we realize the dazzling array we would receive from fresh voices who introduced us to the children and youth featured within this collection.

As you read these stories, you'll see that helping NC's children and youth—and keeping America's Promise to them—takes many exemplary forms. There are great examples of parents who ensure that their children get necessary services ("Wheels of Steel," "Josh—A Gift From the Community") and those parents who persevere and make things happen ("Never Settle for Less Than Their Best," "One Mother's Challenge"). Some are stories of homegrown communities of caring that crop up—from a mentoring program in Gates County down east ("GENESIS: The Coming into Being") to a one-man effort in Raleigh to create a sense of community resembling the one he grew up in a generation ago in Philadelphia ("Larry's Kids").

And, of course, there are fresh instances of tried and true programs such as Community Based Alternatives in Durham ("Hope, Love, Charity... and Basketball") and Boy Scouts ("For Himself, His Community and His Country") that work.

All 22 stories incorporate service to children and families and reflect one or more of the five America's Promises:

1)  An ongoing relationship with a caring adult,
2)  Safe places and structured activities during non-school hours to learn and grow,
3)  A healthy start and a healthy future,
4)  A marketable skill through effective education,
5)  An opportunity to give back through community service.

Every story presents a compelling example of how at least one of these five Promises to children is or is not being kept by adults across North Carolina, celebrates the diversity of NC's children and provides a starting point for dialogue about good communities for children, youth and families. What does your community need to more fully deliver on these Promises? What is already underway in your community that can be adapted and built upon elsewhere in North Carolina?

Service to community is an American idea that runs deep in the Tarheel State. We will continue our work at the state level, but will vigorously promote volunteerism as an essential local strategy for improving quality of life—for those of you who volunteer, as well as for the children and youth who benefit from the service given. This volume stands as a tribute to this noble concept and an invitation to all North Carolinians to *join up*.

*—Alton R. Anderson, MD*  *—Linda H. Harrill*
*Chair, NCCAI Board of Directors*  *President, CISNC*

# *Editor's Note*

When the NC Child Advocacy Institute asked me to edit a raw collection of essays on North Carolina's children, I was hesitant and even skeptical. I wondered how we could bring life to young faces and programs with such random samples. The laughter, passions, resilience and enthusiasm of children are difficult to capture in snapshots, as these brief portraits must necessarily be. I was also dubious about the challenge that the contributors — most of whom are not professional writers or journalists — would face in presenting these children not as portraits, but as living, moving, growing, young people.

But curiosity convinced me to take on the project. Driving through North Carolina's counties, I have often been struck by the sight of a young figure walking along a rural road, riding a bike near a playground, or playing basketball on the cemented pavement of a housing project. At gas stations, I have lost many minutes watching children dig into their pockets for a few more cents to complete the purchase of a grape

Slurpee, a Pepsi freeze, or Cheerwine soda with bag of chips, a box of Nerds, or a stick of beef jerky. Mostly, I see only their backs. But the faces glimpsed for a moment through a car window or a chance encounter — some smiling, others frowning, still others worn beyond their years — leave me wondering for miles who the child is, and what his or her life is like, where he had come from, where she was going. Through this project, I've been given the virtual experience of meeting those children, and I've been enriched by it.

The adults who help the children in this collection of stories have inspired me almost as much as the young people themselves. The 11-year-old Chinese student in Concord, struggling to assimilate, and his fifth grade teacher who includes the student in her family outings. The young Bosnian refugee family in Charlotte, their nightmares still not behind them, and the teacher whose Vietnam experiences allow him to understand and ease the children's trauma.

The reflection of these children in their adult author's eyes is just as impressive. Elizabeth Warren writes of mentoring a Raleigh teenage mother, little younger than herself, seeking a high school diploma and a better life for her son. Young people whose bodies are stricken by cerebral palsy and confined to wheel chairs, but whose determination to do their best remains truly inspirational. Accounts from journalists of children being schooled in juvenile facilities, of living through foster care, are just as effective in bringing to life the worlds of these young people.

Most remarkable are the snatches of scenes in these stories that come from the heart, their words merging into beautiful and haunting images. I won't forget the way Kay Windsor gently brushed her daughter's eyelids, forever giving her dreams. Nor will I forget Claudia Russell's adopted daughter being rescued — small, malnourished and terrified — from a closet and then from the mental institution which was to become her home. Russell's nutrition, nurture, and love brought out a loving and trusting child in the traumatized girl whom social workers and doctors had thought was too retarded to function in the real world. Russell and her adopted daughter proved them wrong.

Each piece is written with a different voice. They speak not only of the child, but of their adult authors. Each story has its own strengths and insights. A priority in my editing was to retain the powerful authenticity of the authors' voices. What I hope emerges from this collection is the same wonderful collage of faces, lives and experiences that came to me by e-mail, fax and disk. They had more texture and breadth to them than I had ever thought to look for. The care, love, and hope they are written with are more telling than most polished articles I read. I never anticipated enjoying this project so much, nor did I anticipate learning so much. I hope you learn as much as I did, in whatever ways the authors touch you—because they're bound to touch us all in different ways. I hope you take away some of the smiles and tears of our children and in the process you see how impressionable and colorful, wise and innocent, resilient and optimistic North Carolina's children are. Whether they face poverty, tragedy or loss, or bask in honors and successes, you can't help feeling their brightness.

*—Jennifer Toth*

# Contents

≈⌒≈

# Never Settle for Less
# Than Their Best

## Claudia Russell

⇒◡⇐

I had been a foster mother for only a couple of months when a social worker called to ask if I would take in a little girl almost five years old, named Myra.* She told me that she had found the child in a closet in rural western North Carolina, and that the little girl was retarded. Myra was to be placed in one of our state institutions when she was old enough, according to her case plan. In the meantime, the social worker was looking for a foster care home to take Myra. Children had to be six years old to be institutionalized at that time.

When Myra arrived at our home, she was malnourished. She had a large, distended belly, delayed language development, and was afraid of almost everything. Right away I fell

---

*Claudia Russell has cared for over 130 children in her 18 years as a foster parent. From 1979 to 1981, Mrs. Russell was a house parent for the Baptist Children's Home. She has one daughter and three sons ages 10 to 30; and five grandchildren ranging in age from nine months to eight years. She is currently the Ministry Assistant at Love Memorial Baptist Church in Goldsboro.*

1

in love with her. The little blond ringlets that clung close to her face, her sky blue eyes, and very fair complexion went straight to my heart.

The first couple of days Myra was in our home she watched us very closely. I would find food she had hidden in her clothes drawers and under her bed. Not things like cookies and snacks but biscuits, fruit or pieces of meat. She was storing up for later, just in case there wouldn't be enough. Most of the time she sat in a rocking chair, rocking so that the chair hit the wall. When I would move the chair so it wouldn't hit the wall she would sit still, wait for me to leave the room, and then move the chair back and resume rocking.

When I gave her a bath she would whine and cry: "Please, don't hurt me." It broke my heart. Many of those early days I cried and prayed as I bathed and dressed her. But as time passed, she drew to the gentleness I felt toward her and even began to voice her appreciation.

"Oh, thank you, Mommie, for giving me a bath and washing my hair," she would say. Or, "Thank you, for a clean bed to sleep in." She would also run around the house as I cooked a meal, shouting, "Mommie's cooking supper!!"

One day I took Myra shopping to buy a dress for Sunday school. It was just a plain simple dress. To watch her, you would have thought it was the finest dress in the world. At the check out when she realized that we were taking the dress home she yelled "Hooray!!" at the top of her voice. And when Myra saw what Santa had brought her the first Christmas she was with us, she kept backing up and asking, "Is it really all mine?" There were so many things that we took for granted that Myra saw as very special.

Myra and I spent lots of time cuddling and rocking, dressing baby dolls, singing songs, and just enjoying being together. Myra became my little helper and stuck right by my side. My husband and I already had two sons when Myra came to us.

The oldest was two-and-a-half years old. Our youngest was 13 months and had cerebral palsy. Our baby became Myra's favorite plaything. She saw me rub his back when he was fussy, so every time she heard him whimper she would run to him and rub his back. It was such a joy to watch her learn caregiving skills and trust with him. She would talk to him and he to her. Much of what was said we couldn't understand, but they understood each other with their hearts.

As the months passed it became time for Myra to be re-evaluated at Western Carolina Center. When the doctors saw Myra, they were amazed by the change in her. She was much more like little girls her age than they had ever dreamed possible. Her social worker and I had been laughing just the week before about how Myra imitated everything she saw me do.

Myra and I spent time each day coloring and writing the alphabet or counting. I taught her to count her crayons and then realized that she thought the numbers we were saying were really the names of the crayons. We also spent time learning daily living skills. All of the children in our home had simple chores to do such as making their beds, picking up their toys, putting their clothes in the proper place, and so forth. Each child also had a responsibility to the family and was expected to help set the table, fold clothes, vacuum the living room, or whatever additional tasks needed to be done. With these chores, I was trying to teach the children that family members take care of each other, not just themselves.

When Myra started school, we decided to place her in kindergarten, instead of first grade. School was a real challenge for her at first. It was difficult for her to follow the rules and sometimes she didn't want to leave me. She began speech class early in school, which was a great help to everyone. Thanks in part to the school speech pathologist and the help we gave her at home, it became much easier to understand what she was saying. I would tell her that if she wanted something, she would have to tell me what she wanted, not just show me. She would try so hard and I rewarded her every effort.

My husband and I attended training sessions offered by Social Services and other state agencies so we could learn how to better help special needs children. I read everything I could get my hands on. I learned that love isn't always meek and mild. For Myra to survive this world, she would have to become tough. So at times, I was tough on her. I encouraged her in areas where she didn't want to change or learn something new. She didn't want to learn to ride a bicycle, but I put her on one and held her up and ran beside her until she could do it all by herself. When she was able to ride it herself, she was so happy. "Oh, thank you, Mommie," she told me jumping up and down. "I really do like to ride my bike."

Many learned skills went much the same way. She would resist, and I would push, knowing all the time her trust for me was growing. But there were also many times I just fell on my face before the Lord and asked for His help because I didn't know what to do. The Lord was always there for me, giving me encouragement, sending someone or something to give me hope. I thought about how Anne Sullivan had pushed Helen Keller and that helped give me the courage to keep pushing. Though sometimes Myra would resist when I pushed her, more often she tried because she was learning that I would always be there for her. And I was often rewarded watching her figure her way through a task. She didn't always go about a task the same way most others would, but she ended up at the same place and that is what counted.

Myra quickly became part of our family. Our boys thought of her only as their sister. After four years, Social Services cleared her for adoption and we were allowed to legally take her as our own. It was such a special time for our family. She kept telling us that she wanted to be

"Daddy's Angel." I discovered that she heard me tell some-one that we had picked out the name Angela for one of our sons if he had been a girl, so that is who she wanted to be. We assured her that we loved her no matter what her name was, and that she was our little girl.

Those early teen years can be so difficult for any child and it was no different for Myra. In the ninth grade her grades were terrible. I always told the children that if a "C" was their best then I was happy with a "C," but if that was not their best then I would tell them: "Let's not settle for less than your best." Myra had so many questions about who she was and what she would grow up to be like. When I questioned her about her problems at school, she answered honestly.

"I don't want to go to high school because that will mean that I'll soon graduate and have to leave home," she told me. I assured her that she would not have to leave home just because she graduated. That was not the way things went in this family. When other teenagers talked about how they hated their parents and wanted to leave home, it really troubled her. Many nights she and I would talk about things she was con-cerned about until the early morning hours. I was so thank-ful for the love and trust between the two of us. Even as a teenager, Myra always said that I was her best friend. When she would go out with her friends or on a date and returned home, she would come to her daddy's and my bed and cuddle with me, telling me all about her night out.

Myra did graduate from high school and then went on to attend Wayne Community College in Goldsboro where she graduated with an Associate Degree in Medical Transcription. After graduation from college, she went to work at our local hospital. She now does medical transcription in an office for three doctors.

From the time we began to think of Myra as our little girl, I prayed that she would find a loving mate. I knew that God

had a very special man in mind for her. I prayed for God to develop in him the kind of character that would meet Myra's needs. In late 1988, one of our church friends asked me if Myra was dating anyone special because she had a nephew that she wanted to introduce to her. After Tal* and Myra were introduced and had spent some time together Myra came to me and said, "Momma, there is something special about this guy and I want to get to know him." Well, she did get to know him. They continued dating and by summer it was obvious to everyone they were very much in love.

Myra was working at the hospital during this time, and often worked second shift. Many evenings, Tal would come to our house and wait for Myra to get off work at midnight. He and I became close friends during this time because we talked about all kinds of things while he waited for her. He would drive to the hospital and follow her home to make sure she got home safely. They married in the fall of 1989. Tal is such a tender man and he loves Myra so much. I know that he is the man we prayed for all those years. It is such a great blessing for your children to grow up and really love you, but when their spouses love you, it is a double blessing. They now have a son and two little girls. They both are very good parents and are doing a wonderful job teaching their children love and respect.

I look at Myra now as a young mother and I am so proud of her. She really is a wonderful mother and it is truly an enormous blessing that we share such a good relationship. I could have searched the whole world over and not found a more perfect daughter. I think of the frightened little girl who came to me so long ago and Myra doesn't resemble her at all. It makes cold chills run all over me to think of where she would be today if that social worker had not found her so long ago.

My husband and I were foster parents for eighteen years. We became the first foster home in Wayne County to be licensed for special needs children. Myra and our boys saw many children come and go as we cared for over 130 children. One day when our oldest son was four, he asked me when he would be getting a new Mommie and Daddy. You see, even he could not tell which children were fostered and which were not. We loved all those children with all the love we had. I think that is one of the things we were able to teach Myra. We loved her unconditionally. Not because she was flesh of our flesh but because she was herself a precious creation of God. I am sure that God used all those children in our care to help Myra learn care-giving skills. There were times when our house was overflowing with children and lots of hands were needed for any task to be completed. Those children also helped Myra see that she was not the only child to whom terrible things had happened.

There were times when it was just the five of us, and we made good use of those times too. We did special things together that we were not able to do when we had a house full of children. We'd go to the movies or go to a special place to eat. One Saturday morning we decided on the spur of the moment to go to the beach. We had such a good time and even now we talk about that day and the great fun we had feeding the sea gulls. Those times also helped us see our family in a different light than most families see themselves. We knew we were a unit and it took each one of us to make the family complete. We believe that we were called by God to care for hurting children. Each child that came to our home brought new challenges and lessons for us to learn. I believe that no child came to our home and left the same, just as we were never the same for knowing them. They left a piece of themselves with us and took a part of us with them.

I watch Myra with her little ones now and I can see her doing many of the things we did together. It is important to Myra to spend special time with each of her children every day, reading, cuddling, rocking and praying. She has begun to instill in her children that the family works together and that it takes each one to make the family complete. She says one of the greatest things she learned and wants to pass on to her children is that trust is built through honesty. Her youngest little girl looks so much like Myra did as a child. I can see in her gestures, as well as her looks, so much of her Mommie.

Thankfully, I don't see the hurt and injury that Myra brought with her when she came to us. I guess I really see what Myra could have been like if she had not gone through the things she did. An end has come to that line of abuse, the chain has been broken. That is what we wanted to accomplish most of all. For Myra to feel loved and to teach her trust and to love in return — if that is the measuring stick for my life — then I can say I have been successful. ☞

* The names used are not the real names of my daughter and her husband.

# Shock Waves: A Bosnian Family Resettles in North Carolina

## Barbara Thiede

⋙⋘

P sychologists call them "beacons" — people who help save traumatized children simply by being there for them, by staying put and staying constant.

Without them, a child may survive. With them, children have havens where haunting memories of famine or torture, war or death do not perpetually dominate their lives.

Seventeen-year-old Aldin and 12-year-old Aldina Kulovac are lucky survivors of the war in Bosnia. They still have both their parents and an aunt, uncle, and cousins nearby. Educational and social institutions in America have also provided them with beacons.

The Kulovacs survived the war in Bosnia — but not before they witnessed evil. The entire family emigrated to the

_Barbara Thiede spent too many years pursuing her Ph.D. in comparative German and American history. Now she works too many jobs. Among them are public relations writer and freelance journalist, personal columnist for_ The Charlotte Observer's _regional bi-weekly, "Cabarrus Neighbors," and coordinator for the 1999 Reed Gold Mine Bicentennial. She has been married for 16 years and has one son._

United States between 1996 and 1997.

They now live in a country that largely ignored the genocidal war against Bosnian Muslims. Most Americans know little about the war, although most can call up a dim memory, a half-formed association defined by words like "atrocities" or "war crimes."

Still, America's teachers care about the refugee children in their classrooms, even if they are not always familiar with the events that drove them here. They have become beacons for the children not because of a passionate interest in world history, but because the children's needs are written on their young, worn faces.

Only the Kulovacs know their story. They do not speak of it openly, partly because they don't know the English words for their past yet. But mostly they keep their past in silence because they want to forget as much of the horror as possible. Because they want to start over, they try to forget. They tell fragments of their story now, to bring light to North Carolina's refugee children better.

In 1995, the Serbs had surrounded the small town of Zepa. Families tried to send someone out each night; everyone was hoping humanitarian aid would literally fall from the skies.

But when the packages fell, they brought out the snipers. Finding food to survive became deadly.

Nezim Kulovac is a short and wiry man whose squarish face is deeply lined. He and his then 14-year-old son, Aldin, endured many long waits for relief-bearing planes that never showed up. Mostly, though, Nezim went alone.

Each time, Aldin's mother, Hidajeta, and his nine-year-old sister, Aldina, stayed up, worrying whether Nezim and Aldin would bring anything home. They tried to assume that they would come home at all.

During the war, the Kulovacs lived in an environment

ruled by death: death by starving, death by shelling, death by torture, death by rape. Rape hotels reminded the world of the Korean "comfort women." Concentration camps and mass graves reminded the world of the Killing Fields in Cambodia, and Auschwitz in Nazi Germany.

Bodies of Muslim women and girls were found on the streets, thrown on the roadsides after Serbian soldiers were finished with them. Pictures of Bosnian men, starved and skeletal, looked out of magazine covers at a largely indifferent audience.

The world outside Bosnia seemed unable to comprehend these horrors. The Serbians had launched a genocidal war, even if Western governments refused to use the word.

One day, Hidajeta was at home with her two children when their house was hit by a powerful grenade. When Hidajeta walked out the door, she and the children saw the bodies of neighbors lying in their yard.

Soon after, the Serbs captured Zepa. Women and children were driven out by the Serbs on bus convoys. Hidajeta, Aldin, and Aldina rode out of the town, passing their home for the last time.

The men of the captured town had to make a run for it. Nezim ran, but the Serbs found him soon after and sent him to Sljivovica, a concentration camp.

For three months, Hidajeta and the children did not know whether Nezim had survived. Then came a message. The Red Cross had come to Sljivovica and gave prisoners the opportunity to write to their families.

"On the days that they [the family] received messages," Hidajeta explained through Dino Ajanovic, who works as a translator and case manager for Charlotte's Refugee Resettlement Office, "Aldina would be the one to cry the most."

When Hidajeta sat down with her two children at a meal, she remembers her daughter asking, "what does my father eat now?"

Aldina remembers too, looking down at her thin hands. Her long, golden hair is pulled back from her pale face, and when she closes her green eyes, the shadows under them appear almost purple. She sits quietly, too slender to make a dent in the sofa.

Nezim spent six months in the concentration camp — worrying. He had reason to. As early as 1992, American media was reporting specific and conclusive information on the Serbian policy of "ethnic cleansing." Serbian soldiers revealed that they were ordered to take Muslim women and girls from rape hotels and not to return them. Americans had plenty of evidence that Serbian war aims were more than simply territorial — that they included eradicating the Bosnian Muslim population.

Hidajeta and the children stayed in Visoko, near Sarajevo. After three months of sporadic messages, she heard that Nezim and his brother had been given the opportunity to emigrate by the Office of the United Nations High Commissioner for Refugees.

The men were given a choice of potential locations. They chose America. Nezim's case was taken over by the United States Catholic Conference. The USCC is based in New York and tries to resettle refugees where they may already have family members. If they have no family already located in the U.S., the USCC sends refugees where they can best serve them.

Nezim was sent to Charlotte in the summer of 1996, where he was met by a case manager working with the Refugee Resettlement Office of Catholic Social Services. The Refugee Resettlement Office receives notices of the arrival of refugees through its parent organization, the USCC. Since 1979, the Charlotte office has settled nearly 7,000 refugees from Vietnam, Cambodia, Laos, Poland, Russia, Armenia, Ethiopia, Liberia, Somalia, Cuba, and other nations. Among them have been about 250 Bosnians.

The Refugee Resettlement Office case manager is responsible for preparing files, filling out necessary paperwork, and finding and furnishing housing. Two employment specialists work on finding jobs for the refugees. Children are enrolled at area schools within ten days after arriving in Charlotte. But even with the resettlement office's help, there were difficulties. Although the family was classified as refugee, Hidajeta and the children were not granted the usual eight months of Medicaid from the Department of Social Services. Nezim, apparently, made too much money cleaning carpets. His family was not eligible.

It took well over a year of work on both sides of the world before Hidajeta and the two children were allowed to join Nezim in Charlotte. Hidajeta and the children arrived in February 1997, and the family settled in a narrow, two-bedroom apartment. Affordable housing is hard to find in Charlotte — harder if you happen to be a refugee.

"They say: 'We have to have a credit check,'" says Ajanovic, the interpreter. But refugees, as most apartment owners know, aren't likely to arrive in America with a Mastercard or Visa in their pockets.

Nezim changed jobs and began working in a factory in Gastonia, making plastic spools for thread. He works the night shift 56 hours a week and hasn't had a day off in the year he's worked at the factory. Hidajeta got a job working at a laundry, where she works 40 hours a week, and can't imagine when she might find the time to learn a little English.

Both Nezim and Hidajeta miss their old jobs in Bosnia. Nezim had worked for the post office for 13 years. Hidajeta worked as a secretary, and later as a teacher for elementary children up to the fourth grade.

Ajanovic enrolled Aldin and Aldina in school almost immediately. Then they began the difficult process of learning in a completely foreign language.

Everyone in the family had learned some Russian in Bosnia, but no one in the family read, understood, or spoke English. Aldina does remember taking English for one short month, but learning numbers one through 10 could not have been much preparation for the fifth grade homework she took home from an American school.

Aldin had been a straight-A student in Bosnia. In America, he could no longer simply communicate what he had absorbed from his classwork. He had to learn to communicate, first.

The children came to Charlotte with two academic advantages: they were both literate in their own languages and they had received the benefit of disciplined and demanding schooling in their own country.

In Bosnia, Aldin says, he had to answer exam questions in his own words. No multiple choice, no fill-in-the-blank. He finds American tests easy by comparison.

Aldin bites his fingernails almost absentmindedly, sitting in jeans and a t-shirt, his body positioned like a concave mirror on the sofa. He is thin and short, and carries himself with the stoop of an insecure teenager or a child who is hiding something.

One of Aldin's teachers at Independence High School, Janet Stravino, points out that some of her English as a Second Language students have never had any formal education. For some kids, she says, a multiple choice test is as foreign as the food.

"It takes weeks, weeks, weeks," Stravino says of learning how to take a multiple choice test. "They'll circle number one [each time], they'll circle one word. They have no idea."

In Aldin and Aldina's case, however, the educational structure was similar. Their teachers have been satisfied with their adjustment to the American educational system.

"For Aldin," says ESL teacher Karen Brown, "education is important."

Aldin was one of a few Bosnian students at his school, so he was not completely isolated. In fact, he befriended one other Bosnian teenager and helped tutor him through the school year.

"Any time a student becomes a teacher," says Brown, "it helps."

Still, Aldin tends to be a quiet student, and his teachers must push him to speak freely, unless he is in his history class.

"In reading and writing he won't say a word," says Kevin Whitsun, Aldin's English and social studies teacher. "In history he's on the ball. He always participates in class. He gives the answers."

Aldin doesn't volunteer much information about his background, though. In a "History of My Life," an essay that he wrote for Whitsun seven months after he arrived in America, he is specific about present realities, not past ones.

"Today I live in Charlotte," he writes. "My apartment is in Green Oaks Lane. My apartment has two bedrooms and I don't like my apartment. I like American school . . . I came to America because in my country is war.

"After colege [sic] and school I want good job and go back in my country. Go to my country make me sooo [sic] happy."

Aldin's mother says he is a quiet child by nature who tends to hide his emotions. But Aldin has made an effort to put his experience in perspective by reading about other children who were separated from their fathers but later rejoined them. He says such books help him feel less alone.

Still, Hidajeta knows that Aldin will not forget seeing corpses in their yard. When she thinks back, her nearly turquoise eyes are hooded. She tucks her feet under her long skirt.

She hopes Aldina will forget, she says.

Aldina says she misses her Bosnian friends. She writes them, and telephones now and then.

Dr. Joe Marlin Riggs, one of her ESL teachers at Eastway

Middle School, describes Aldina as a responsible student. Like Aldin, she does her homework. Like Aldin, she copes partly by paying attention to the needs of other refugee students.

"If she doesn't understand something, she doesn't hesitate to ask," Riggs says. "One of the striking things about Aldina is that she is so willing and capable of helping others. There are two other sixth grade girls and one sixth grade boy that have come here in the last month. She's one of the reasons they feel so at home because she is their mentor."

Dr. Riggs, a Vietnam War veteran, deliberately avoids asking his students about their past lives, although he is more than willing to listen if they volunteer information.

"I don't want to talk about it and cause flashbacks," he explains.

The children's teachers are used to worrying about their students, because at any time, they may find themselves in a minefield of traumatic past experiences.

Riggs once sent a letter home about a boy who hadn't made progress at school. A fellow Bosnian student wrote Riggs back, explaining that he was writing because the parents couldn't. His fellow student, he explained, had witnessed some of the worst Serbian war crimes. He had seen members of his immediate family maimed, tortured, and killed. He had been unable to go to school in Bosnia for years before he came to America.

"You can't judge a student like that with the same yardstick," Riggs says. So he gives that student extra responsibilities, and praises every small achievement. He hopes that a budding sense of security and growing self-confidence will translate into academic progress.

Even when they know very little about their students' pasts, ESL teachers at Independence High School and Eastway Middle are always looking for ways to be beacons, to be involved with their students on a variety of levels. At both schools, teachers routinely make "house calls" each week, visiting students and their families in their homes.

Every week, ESL teachers chat with parents. Sometimes they take the students to the mall or to a movie. Kevin Whitsun bargained with the Charlotte Transit Authority and received two free passes for his students.

"They need someone to show them around," he says.

The teachers watch and wonder how best to understand each student on his or her own terms. Many of Aldin's teachers note that he is exceptionally quiet most of the time, but they believe that part of his silence is due to his introspective character.

Dr. Riggs sits near Aldina in the cafeteria and worries a little because, he says, Aldina doesn't seem to have much appetite.

The children are aware that their teachers care. Aldin says all his "professors" have taken an interest in him. Mr. Whitsun, he says, is planning to publish the stories the students are writing about their lives.

The children have friends at school: friends their own age who have come from their own country, and friends in American teachers who visit and watch over them.

The children know that their case manager, who lives in the same apartment complex, is there to help. The Kulovacs, Ajanovic says (and he explains to them, too, what he has said), could complain about him any time to his own boss, because she regularly visits the family too.

The parents have a specific goal in mind: to make sure the children get a good education. They would like to go back to Bosnia, they say, but they think the children are safer here.

So Hidajeta visits the school and talks as best she can to Dr. Riggs. Nezim works hard in the spool factory and says the children do the same in school. He didn't expect them to do so well given the language barrier.

The past lives with them, though — as it does with every Bosnian Muslim who survived the war.

Ajanovic, the Kulovac's case manager and translator, explains Aldin's feelings about the war.

"He says, 'It's hard to forgive.'" But Ajanovic must correct himself. He has mistranslated; his tongue has slipped over the word he wants to a word that makes equal sense. "It's hard to FORGET what was going on."

In the brief discussion that follows, Aldin agrees that "forgive" is just as applicable.

Before the war, Hidajeta says, she loved everything about Bosnia. Before the war, Nezim says, those years were the best of his life.

They both wish they could take the war out of their children's lives, out of their pasts. But they know it's impossible. They can't get the war out of their own heads.

Nezim "tries to hide it somewhere," Ajanovic translates. "Most of the time it comes to [Hidajeta] when she is working — she doesn't think she can get away from that."

The house they had. The bodies lying in the yard. The search for food. The convoy driving past home. Running away.

A family torn apart is together, but not whole. They have each other, so they have a haven. They have friends, so they have help. The children can look to teachers they can trust. They have a future.

But their havens will never be entirely free from the shock waves of war. ☞

# *Wheels of Steel*

## E d   B r i s t o l

≈

The young driver's ed student was discouraged.

Driving a car is every teen's consuming passion. It's freedom-on-wheels, a way to put life's tribulations, for the moment, in your rear-view mirror. For this high school sophomore, born with a physical disability, driving held out for once the special promise of relatively effortless, unfettered movement.

But she was worried. Driving still has its physical challenges, and what if she wasn't up to it? That day in driver's ed class, her physical therapist had come to consult with her driving teacher. Her future as a driver was in their hands.

Her therapist, Charlotte Hughes, had brought along a friend, home from college on spring break. A couple of years earlier, the young man had been North Carolina's Athlete of

*Ed Bristol, a Raleigh writer, is the marketing/public relations director of Easter Seals of North Carolina and president of Bristol Associates, a public relations firm serving nonprofit and for-profit clients. He has 20 years of experience in media, advertising and public relations.*

the Year, and, for three years running, the winner of Orange County High School's Scholar/Athlete Award. He'd been on the wrestling team, and remained an avid basketball player, water skier, and horseman.

Right now he was headed in the direction of the young would-be driver. Hughes knew that 18-year-old Shawn Hessee could reassure the girl. She knew, because her friend and former client — diagnosed as an infant with cerebral palsy and now carefully maneuvering his power wheelchair — had been there.

Breaking down barriers is what his son likes best, says Layne Hessee of Hillsborough.

"What Shawn doesn't have in physical ability with his legs," says Layne, "he has turned into a drive to accomplish just about anything he's wanted to do."

Like rappelling down a 15-foot wall. Or playing on a nationally ranked wheelchair basketball team. Or water skiing on a specially-made ski.

"When he was little, I would fasten him in an old inner tube and pull him along at about 60 miles per hour," Layne laughs. "The harder he'd hit that water, the better he'd like it."

"He's tough. Shawn's always had a high tolerance for pain." But more softly, Layne adds, "Maybe it's because of all the surgeries he's had."

How many surgeries? "Counting the tubes in his ears," says his mother, Donna Hessee, "anywhere from 13 to 20," including the time he was in a half-body cast, the procedure on the back of his legs, and when they redirected some of his salivary flow down his throat to eliminate the drooling sometimes characteristic of spastic diaplegia. That's the condition with which he was diagnosed shortly after he was adopted by Donna and Layne.

"He was three, just turning four," recalls Donna. "We knew there was a possibility that he'd never walk."

The Hessees remained hopeful. "Sometimes he'd take off and go the length of the room," says Layne. "Some of the happiest moments I can remember are when he took his first steps in his walker. We actually saw him in a vertical position instead of crawling on the floor. It was a great moment."

But after working very hard for Shawn's first 14 years, Donna says, "we began working on being OK with him not being able to walk."

The Hessees' version of coming to terms with a limitation only meant redirecting the wealth of natural ability they saw in their son. They weren't about to let him off easy, and it was clear that Shawn was just as determined not to let a thing like not being able to walk get in his way.

Take the time he learned to ride his tricycle. He was six. "He had to work so much harder to do these little ordinary things that kids do," Donna says "but the joy is indescribable when you see him reach that accomplishment."

Or take his high school wrestling career. His dad jokes that he had a perfect record: he never won a match. But on a few occasions, his opponent just couldn't manage to pin him. "He would just lock those arms and they couldn't turn him over," recalls Layne. "He had a strong desire to be on that mat, and even though he would always lose, the look in his eyes after every match told you he was the real winner."

"And 98 percent of his matches ended in a big hug from his opponent," Donna adds. "He's always had a look in his eye that just grabs people. We say he 'beams' people."

Shawn and his parents agree that the defining moment of his young life was his summer camp experience that brought him two first-ever achievements by someone with a disability. It would also bring him to the life-changing conviction that his only true limits would come from within.

When he was eight, his parents discovered Camp Easter in the Pines, operated by Easter Seals of North Carolina for children with disabilities like Shawn's. Shawn remembers clearly that first summer:

"Because I was physically a little bit different from other kids, I was scared. But after I got there, I felt more comfortable because when I was with kids that had a disability, I actually started to participate. I was like 'Wow, this is great!' I'm actually part of a group, a set of friends I could play with. It was a week when I didn't have to worry about helping kids understand me."

"My favorite activity was the dances," Shawn says. It was the kind of event where he had always felt out of place before.

But for all the newfound ease and confidence around other people with disabilities, Shawn felt there was something missing. He was ready for his next challenge.

"After a couple of years at Camp Easter, I began to think, 'OK, camp is great but I still have to go back and socialize with people that don't have disabilities.'"

Easter Seals of N.C. had begun to think along the same lines. They closed Camp Easter and began to work with camps across the state, training counselors to work with disabilities and helping camps adapt facilities so that kids with and without disabilities could share the camp experience. Among them was Camp Hanes, where Shawn faced challenges he hadn't faced at Camp Easter.

"You had to work harder to approach people and make the extra effort to participate with people who didn't understand your situation," he says. Facing this new challenge brought mixed results: "Sometimes I was excited that I had made a difference, that people thought, 'Hey, this kid in the wheelchair is pretty cool.' But then sometimes I thought, 'I've had a tough week.'"

It took both feelings "to keep my fire burning," he says,

and the ember of ambition was growing brighter.

In 1994, 14-year-old Shawn was chosen to represent Camp Hanes at YMCA World Camp. The event brought campers to Charlotte that summer from all over the world, and Shawn — the first person with a disability ever to be chosen World Camp ambassador — made the most of the honor.

"I got to meet people from every corner of the globe and take disability awareness to a worldwide group," he recalls, adding, "I also got to water ski." He was convinced that if he could make it at World Camp, his next goal just might be achievable.

The YMCA counselor-in-training program is tough. Would-be counselors have to be mature, responsible, physically fit, and able to endure the rigors of riding herd on a group of supercharged kids away from home and who, in some cases, would rather not be. Plenty of people without disabilities find they're not up to it. For Shawn, the summer's heat was especially draining.

He remembers that first month-long training as a "whole new world of challenges, working with other people my age who didn't have disabilities and learning, on the same level, how to take care of kids."

With his second summer of training, he became one of the first two people with disabilities ever to complete the program. The experience of "getting out there and showing people what you can do" cemented in his mind what he had always felt in his gut.

"That's when I knew there would always be people who were going to misunderstand me, but that I would always have to keep smiling and doing the best I could. You're going to face adversity, you're going to face difficulty, but somehow you've got to figure out how to come through it.

"Camp gave me the confidence to tell myself, 'Yes, I can do something, I can participate, and I will function in society.'"

Shawn's mom and dad matter-of-factly believe that with

Shawn's "love of people and strong desire to break down barriers, he could succeed in just about anything he tries to do."

In fact, he has become an eloquent public speaker on disability issues. (Donna chuckles that even a childhood chat with Santa Claus ended with a rhetorical flourish. Rejecting a suggested video game as too violent, Shawn stressed that he believed in "peace and goodwill.")

"Speaking is therapeutic for him," says Donna. "He gets a lot of his self-confidence from it."

Shawn sees public speaking as a way to change the world, or at least the way it looks at people with disabilities. Channeling his drive, his desire to remove barriers, his feeling for people, and his dedication to disability issues into speaking, he says, is the fuel that keeps him going.

"I want to be a recharger for people's batteries, to encourage people who feel like giving up," he says. "I was lucky enough to have the right people pushing me at the right time, to mold me into what I am, and I'm going to spend the rest of my life giving that back. I may not be able to reach everybody, but if I can keep somebody from going out and killing somebody, or if I can just help a kid with a disability go to camp, I want to do that."

Does he want to work directly with other people with disabilities? Yes and no, he says. While he continues to get that "tingly feeling" when he helps a kid with a disability, he believes the greater good is to help create a world where there is a single high standard for those with and without disabilities.

"My parents always expected me to perform at the highest level." He had chores to do, he says, and the responsibility "to help out my younger sister, Ashleylayne, and be a good role model for her. They never sat me down and taught me to be tough, but they were always there to support me in some tough times. I respect them the most because they pushed me, they were confident that I could succeed. At the same time they might have been fearful that I couldn't, but they put away that fear."

A good example, Shawn says, is when he went away to East Carolina University in the fall of 1997. How would he adjust there on his own? He still needed help to get dressed. It sometimes took him hours. How would he manage?

By the start of school, the Hessees had hired someone to help get Shawn dressed in the morning and ready for bed at night, but that didn't work out. Worried that providing for the most routine of needs now threatened his college career, they called Shawn. He told them he'd handle it. He recruited a committed coterie of friends to give him a hand morning and night.

But what about his school work? "He made the dean's list his first semester," says Donna.

While proud of his clearing a first big academic hurdle, the Hessees have no illusions that the rest of Shawn's stay at college will be as smooth. With only minimal use of his legs and limited range and strength in his arms, something as mundane as getting dressed is still a big issue.

"Have you ever spent hours giving something every ounce of energy you've got and you still couldn't do it?" Shawn asks. Struggling to get on a single sock once took him two hours.

And it's not much easier for him now than when he was younger. Donna recalls that it would take him 45 minutes to get his shirt on. "It was pretty agonizing. There was a lot of screaming going on for a while, and under the pressure of getting ready for school, it was always worse.

"Of course, I always made him do those things himself," Donna laughs. "Down at school he's got his friends to help."

In high school when he was finally able to dress himself, his parents threw a party with his teachers and friends to celebrate.

Now that Shawn's settled in at college, says Layne, "he'd like to get a car down there." It would not only make life physically easier, it would also improve his social life.

After all, says Shawn, he has "plans like any young person — to settle down, get married and raise kids." The dating issue, often a difficult one for people with disabilities, produced a brief period of bitterness when he was in high school. His remedy was go into his room one day, close the door, and bare his soul into a tape recorder. Afterward he felt much better. "If you really believe in yourself, no matter how down you get, you can always come out of it," he reflects.

Learning to drive has come as a big challenge. Layne

recalls when he was trying to teach Shawn to drive, tension ran high on the part of student and teacher: "I'd get a little nervous and, when we ran off the road and hit the ditch, I'd get a little critical of him. At one point, he finally threw up his hands and said he just couldn't do it." Layne says that's one of the few times Shawn had lost confidence in himself, but that even that was temporary. "Pretty soon," says Layne "we'd come out of the ditch and we'd go again."

For people with disabilities like Shawn's, driving a car has the special allure of allowing some measure of freedom from the encumbrances of disability. That makes the physical challenges of driving all the more frustrating.

"Here I was 16-years-old, and everybody was picking up driving just like that. Everything had always been harder for me, and I was really hoping that just once I could pick up on something really easily and be able to travel around anywhere I wanted to without much physical difficulty."

Even though he has his driver's license and has worked his way beyond several of the adaptive devices he had earlier required, the frustration toward learning to drive with less difficulty endures. Is there ever a time when he thinks he might not be able to pull it off? "That goes through my mind all the time . . ." he replies.

That day in driver's ed class, Shawn was busy calming the young girl's anxieties over learning to drive. He explained how adaptive devices could go a long way to help her maneuver herself and her car safely. Within minutes, the conversation had turned her fears to laughter. As Shawn maneuvered his power chair back to join his physical therapist friend, the would-be driver was now sitting more confidently behind the wheel, ready to get on with the heady business of freedom. Shawn Hessee had "beamed" her. ⤙

# A Promise of Forever

## R o s e   H o o p e r

≈⊃⊂

I f you are a little girl of nine, even the smallest incidents
at school can mushroom to such magnitude that your
entire day seems miserably without promise. But even
your worst days could be better than the best days of a foster
child.

Take just yesterday for instance. You promised yourself you
would study, but first thing that morning at school, you failed
an important math test. At lunch, Katie, who promised to be
your forever best friend sat with someone else in the cafeteria. Then in the hallway, some eighth graders bullied you,
even though you promised yourself you weren't going to let
that happen again. On the bus home, you got grease on your
new pink blouse, and you know your mother is going to have
a fit because you promised her you would be extra careful if
she let you wear it to school today.

*Rose Hooper is features editor for* The Sylva Herald *newspaper in Jackson
County. She first met Jan when doing a story on the growing need for foster
parents in this rural, mountain county.*

28

As soon as you get home, you run to the refuge of your bedroom, slamming the door and the day of unkept promises behind you. Jumping on your bed, you grab your pillow and hug the softness beneath "The Little Mermaid" design. You rub the worn maple post of your small bed — it had rails when you were younger — and feel security in its strength and familiarity.

Lady, the family dog, a honey-colored spaniel and your longtime companion, sneaks in your room, climbs on the bed with you and licks away your tiny tears of frustration as she snuggles close to console you.

You reach over to your matching maple nightstand and pick up the silver-framed family portrait, knowing that later, after supper, you can share your troubles with your mom and dad and, like they always have before, they will ease away your pain with promises of comfort and help.

Your world in that familiar room is your haven. On the other side of the bedroom door, your parents, who have always been there for you no matter what, extend that haven to the rest of your home.

If you are a foster child like nine-year-old Jan, you don't have the security of a bedroom, or even a home that has been your longtime familiar place of love and retreat. And you don't have parents who will always be your source of guiding strength and unconditional love.

You could be alone, with not even a promise.

Complicated as her life is, Jan's style is simple. Her shoulder-length burnished brown hair is cut in a straight bob. Her favorite outfit is a simple white t-shirt covered by a pair of blue denim overalls which hang loosely on her tiny frame. She wears no jewelry — not even pierced earrings — and no nail polish on her closely-clipped nails.

When their mother died, Jan and her older brother Ray went to live with their elderly grandmother, a widow. Their father, a mostly absent figure in their young lives, became even more absent. But life was good for the two youngsters until their grandmother died. Then the two children — Jan was six and Ray was eight — were truly alone.

They had no other family to take them in; their father certainly wouldn't. Suddenly Jan realized that nothing tangible is "for keeps" — not a home or a family.

But Jan was soon to learn that something as intangible as a promise could be "for keeps."

In stepped the Jackson County Department of Social Services, which placed Jan and Ray in the care of foster parents, Steve and Shelly Grindstaff, a young couple married for five years with no children of their own.

Though young, both of the part-time youth ministers sensed immediately that these abandoned, frightened children — Jan especially — longed for a sense of security. Steve and Shelly knew they would probably not remain the children's foster parents permanently. So, how could they give the two children a promise of forever?

"Shelly and I made it our promise to help Jan and Ray develop a strong inner self so no matter what their circumstances in life, they would always have someone to count on — themselves," Steve says.

Ask Jan what was the first thing the Grindstaffs taught her and she will say: "Punishment. Well, not punishment exactly. What I mean is consequences. If I don't do my chores like washing the dishes or emptying the trash, the consequence is that I get more chores."

If Jan, a third grader, doesn't follow her schedule in the morning but "messes around and runs late for school," her consequence is that she has to go to bed early that night.

"If she goes outside before she does her homework, she gets grounded," says Shelly, who matches the consequence to the misbehavior.

"Before, when I did things wrong or bad, I just got spanked," says Jan, tying her soft hair on the top of her head with a rubber band.

Some children don't have anyone to teach them coping skills. Instead, they learn bad behavior. When the going gets tough, if the adults around them deal with it by striking out — either with fists or fistfuls of angry words — that's how the children learn to respond. But when something goes wrong in the Grindstaff household, Jan has learned what to do. "I go straight to Steve or Shelly and tell them if I don't think something is fair."

"I tell Jan to talk it out, rather than act it out," says Steve, who has a sharp wit and a healthy sense of humor. Every comment Jan makes, every action she takes, elicits a quick good-natured response from Steve.

Sometimes when Jan gets angry, she'll pout and say, "Oh, leave me alone."

"When I get like that, Steve tells me to go hit on my pillow," Jan says.

"I always let her know that Shelly and I don't get mad at her, but we get mad at what she does," Steve says.

When she gets mad at other people, Jan writes them letters. With each angry ink stroke, she vents her frustrations. "Oh, I've written some doozy letters, but I never mail them. But that's OK. Just writing them makes me feel better," she explains.

"Jan is a lot like I was when I was a little girl — strong-willed and stubborn," says Shelly, a high-energy lady with bouncing blond hair. "She wants to do what she wants to do when she wants to. Her independent streak is good, but it can put you on some rocky roads."

The foster mother and daughter share "girl talk."

"Shelly understands me pretty well, but she says she can't understand me when I cry so hard that she can't hear the words," Jan says.

"Jan could sing the words, 'Poor, poor pitiful me,' along with Linda Ronstadt," Steve says with a laugh. "In life, everybody has some tough breaks. Jan is no exception. But rather than feeling sorry for herself, we help her concentrate on her strengths."

Her tiny hands — a rubber band can wrap four times around her wrist — are part of Jan's strength. She's taking piano lessons and becoming quite adept at coordinating her left hand in rhythm with her right hand. She's developed a talent for needlepoint and hand stitches and personalizes the presents she gives.

All that angry letter writing has helped Jan with her writing skills. Recently she competed in a writing contest and won a $25 prize. "I wrote about what it was like to be a foster child. I said it made me mad, sad and embarrassed.

"I get mad when people ask me so much. I get embarrassed when people ask me so loud everybody hears. Sometimes when they ask me over and over, I tell them it's none of their business," Jan says. That anger often turns to sadness. "I get sad because it reminds me of my mother and grandmother who are dead. Sometimes when the thought pops in my head about them, I start to cry. But then Steve gets me to talking about something else so it'll pop out of my head."

As a youth minister, Steve knows "that when kids only think about themselves, it can get them in trouble."

"With Jan, I try to get her to concentrate on others. When you take a close look at others, their problems are probably bigger than your problems anyway. So it kind of puts life in perspective and makes your own problems seem smaller."

One way he accomplishes this is by involving her in service projects. Following a recent bad storm — the dwindling tail end of a tornado — Jan helped clean debris and limbs from the grounds of the nearby Broyhill Children's Home. As she picked up tree limbs and carried them to a brush pile, Jan

said it made her feel good. The sheer physical energy invigo-
rated her. Working for the children in the group home made
her feel like she was helping, in her small way. By keeping
busy, she had no time to concentrate on herself or her own
troubles.

Through the Children's Relief Fund, the Grindstaffs sponsor a young South American girl the same age as Jan. It's Jan's
responsibility to prepare the packages for her. "I take a shoe
box and fill it with coloring books and crayons, pencils and
school stuff like that. This last time I put in a little toy racing
car. I thought she might like playing with that," says Jan, who
allocates a portion of her own allowance to purchase these
items. "For $5 she can eat for 21 days. In her country, prices
are cheaper 'cause here at the grocery store you sure can't
get enough food for 21 days with just $5."

This service project, says Steve, helps Jan budget and learn
the value of money, and learn about another country. "Just
as importantly, it helps Jan to concentrate on another young
girl who has less than she does.

"The world doesn't owe you a living," he says. "For some
that's a hard lesson to learn. Any small way I can show Jan
that, even at her young age, will help her in the long run."

Life wasn't always so stable for Jan; it was far more confusing. When she came to live with Steve and Shelly, Jan
would sit on their wooden rail porch looking out over the
Great Smoky Mountains and wonder what would happen if
she lost her brother Ray. "I would get sad thinking about us
ever being separated, but I couldn't stop thinking about it."
Jan didn't share her thoughts with anybody, least of all Ray.
They were her "all alone" thoughts.

Sometimes she would step off the porch and take those
"all alone" thoughts on a walk with her. The Grindstaff's
mountain home, located in a rural section of Jackson
County called Blanton's Branch, afforded Jan an ample

supply of privacy. No neighbors are within eyesight, and only one within earshot.

Steve and Shelly knew Jan needed some space at first. While they were always nearby and within shouting range, they let Jan have her private time. As she walked along the quiet gravel road, Jan could cry freely with no one to see her. She could even sob loudly and no one would hear her. A family of gray squirrels — the only other creatures around — realized this lone girl posed no threat to their sunflower seed supply, so they ignored her as they scampered to raid the bird feeders.

"I kept thinking about Ray being placed in another home, away from me. I didn't want it to happen, but I just decided that if it ever did, I would visit him every day — no matter what."

She kept these thoughts from Ray because her older brother seemed to be adjusting quite well with their foster parents, expecially Steve.

Ray never had a father figure before. His own father was never around and his grandfather died when Ray was very young — long before he and Jan went to live with their grandmother. So Ray took easily to energetic, athletic Steve who pitched ball with him until dark, took him snow skiing and even rollerbladed with him.

Jan watched as Ray would wrestle on the cream-carpeted living room floor with Steve. As she held back, shy and reserved, Jan watched as the two males seemed to bond immediately. At night, after the homework was done, Jan watched as Ray snuggled on the hunter green coach with the couple as they watched television. The three of them looked so comfortable, so cozy together on that overstuffed sofa with the huggable cushions.

But if she let go, if she gave in and joined them, she might get hurt, Jan thought. "Hold back, don't like them, don't love them 'cause you know what happens to people you love," she told herself. They leave you like her father, or they die like her mother and grandmother.

Meanwhile, Steve and Shelly, who plan to continue being foster parents until they start a family of their own, thought about what they could do to help soften Jan's reserve and calm her fears. The couple understood how important Ray was to Jan and how she feared they might be separated. Through DSS, Steve and Shelly secured a court order that the brother and sister would remain together no matter what foster home they were placed in.

When they explained those conditions to Jan, it was like a heavy weight lifting from her tiny shoulders. Somebody had actually known those "all alone" thoughts she was thinking. Moreover, they had acted on them. From the bits of conversation she pieced together, from the Grindstaffs, DSS and her counselors, Jan realized that court action didn't come easily.

For a while, Jan acted like a normal, happy nine-year-old girl with not a care in the world. But that didn't last too long. Jan had already learned nothing is forever, so she thought this good feeling wouldn't last. She began to worry. Troublesome thoughts that she had buried began to surface.

What if her dad suddenly showed up and wanted to take her and her brother away? After all, he was their father, however sorry or absent he was.

"In training as foster parents, the social workers told us in most cases, the ultimate goal is to work with the families through counseling and recovery programs so that the children are eventually placed back in the home," Shelly says. "With Jan and Ray, we knew that was not feasible."

Once again, the couple aided by DSS sought relief through the courts. All parental rights were taken from the father. The action precluded any further threats or ugly battles. It also eased Jan's fears.

Things were going good again. This time, when Jan got to thinking about nothing being forever, no worries or fears surfaced.

"One night I was sitting on the couch watching television and Jan came and plopped on top of me and began cutting up and trying to wrestle with me. It was really annoying. It was right in the middle of my favorite show," Steve jokes as he tells that story in front of Jan. Jan just rolls her eyes, but at the same time, a smile of affection creeps across her face. "Really, I loved it," he confesses, "because I guess that was the moment I knew Jan finally accepted us."

Not long after that, the couple took Jan and Ray to the aquarium in Chattanooga, Tenn., where the family participated in the Discovery Zone experiments with water and its different properties. Jan's favorite activity was stepping into a giant bubble. "You know how you can blow soap bubbles until they get big? Well, this was like the ring you blow them with . . . only you stepped in this big ring and then pulled the bubble up over you. Your whole body was right inside a bubble. It was the coolest thing," Jan says, bubbling with her own excitement.

As Shelly watched Jan pull the prismatic creations around her tiny frame, the foster mother thought about how she could be like that bubble. "I want to protect Jan, to put my arms around her and promise her safety . . . I don't ever want her bubble to burst. Whenever Jan and Ray have to leave us, Steve and I want them to know that we will still be there for them, no matter what."

Jan and Ray have now lived with Steve and Shelly for more than two years. The couple knows the hardest part will come the day the children have to leave.

"We haven't had to let go yet, to experience that pain, but we know it can come at any time. God gave us enough love to have them, and we trust Him to give us enough love to let them go," says Shelly, who calls her foster parent experience "a blessing."

A few weeks ago, a collie-shepherd mixed-breed dog wandered onto the family's wooden rail porch. Wagging her matted tail, the dog affectionately took to Jan, following her every move and eagerly woofing down whatever morsels Jan shared from the kitchen. "I hand fed her hot dogs 'cause that's my favorite food," says Jan who eats her hot dogs plain — "no catsup, no mustard, no pickles, no nothing."

"Do you think we could be her foster parents?" Jan asked Shelly.

"What would that mean, Jan? How would you be a foster parent to a dog?" Shelly asked her foster daughter.

"Well, she doesn't have a home so we would give her one . . . and we would feed her and play with her and take care of her and love her and she would have a happy life," Jan explained from experience.

They kept the dog and they call her "Foster."

Last Christmas, Steve and Shelly received the best gift of all and it wasn't wrapped in green and red under their Fraser fir tree. It happened on a visit to Santa Claus. When Jan walked up to Santa, she didn't rattle off a list of all the presents she wanted him to bring her. Instead, she told Santa, "I have everything I need. I just want the other boys and girls to have a Merry Christmas."

Standing hidden in the background, but close enough to hear Jan's words, Steve was filled with the joy of the season and the moment. He could see a promising future for this little girl. Jan's words filled his heart. ⇒

# Double Oaks:
# Success at School
# Starts Here

**S u s a n     O r r**

≈)⌐

F airview Homes can be a tough neighborhood for kids
to grow up in. Though the public housing complex
sits in the shadow of the Charlotte skyline, less than
two miles from the upscale townhouses of the Fourth Ward
historic district, life at Fairview Homes is a far cry from that
fancy neighborhood. In the summer of 1997, police broke up
a multimillion dollar heroin distribution ring on Statesville Avenue, which runs right by Fairview Homes. When neighborhood children wanted to organize a neighborhood clean-up a
while back, the project had to be scrapped because the adults
in charge decided it would be too dangerous — hypodermic
needles litter the ground along with other trash.

---

*Susan Orr is a staff writer at* The Enquirer-Journal *in Monroe, where she
covers arts and entertainment and health. She has met and written about
all types of people, from artists to inmates to ordinary folks with extraordinary stories to tell. It was as a volunteer with the service group Hands on
Charlotte that she first learned about Double Oaks, the urban family resource
center that is the focus of this story.*

In the midst of these mean streets, the Double Oaks Pre-Kindergarten and Family Resource Center offers a beacon of light for children and families from Fairview Homes and from other neighborhoods in north and west Charlotte. It's located in a residential neighborhood, just across the grassy yard from the faltering homes.

Javonté Truesdale, a five-year-old with large, dark eyes accentuated by long, sweeping eyelashes is among the children who live in Fairview Homes and attend pre-kindergarten at Double Oaks every day. In his denim overalls and wearing an open smile, Javonté is always eager to arrive at the child-friendly building which is surrounded by sidewalks painted with giant letters and numbers. A colorful mural on a wall by the front door depicts the growth of an oak, from tiny acorn to mighty tree.

From 8 a.m. to 2 p.m. Monday through Friday, Javonté and the 446 other children in this inaugural class grow — both academically and socially — by attending pre-kindergarten at Double Oaks. Here they learn the basics which will give them a leg up when they enter kindergarten next year. The building also houses a Family Resource Center, which offers many enrichment programs for neighborhood children and their families.

Double Oaks was originally an elementary school, which the Charlotte-Mecklenburg school system closed in 1981 because of racial integration. Afterward, the school system worked with various community agencies to bring the building new life as a community center.

Double Oaks' pre-kindergarten program started in August 1997, as part of a system-wide effort by the Charlotte-Mecklenburg schools. Along with Double Oaks, the school system has two other stand-alone pre-kindergarten centers — at Plaza Road and Tryon Hills. There are also pre-kindergarten programs at 12 elementary schools. In the first year of the program, 1,850 children began their school careers at one of these pre-kindergartens. Charlotte is one of only a few cities in the state with stand-alone pre-kindergarten programs. Though there are community programs at Charlotte's other pre-kindergartens, Double Oaks is the only one with a fully developed Family Resource Center.

Javonté and his 15 classmates spend their days in classroom A-2, a place filled with colorful learning materials, student work and toys. Separate activity centers for computers, writing, reading, math, science and art are scattered around the room. Each center is set up with educational activities. There are also areas in the classroom where the students can play house or create things with blocks.

One of the most important parts of the room sits along the back wall, a place where, four times a day, Javonté and his classmates gather with their teacher, Jennifer Griggs, to take part in what is known as "literacy circle." At these times, Griggs leads the students in some sort of word-based activity — reading aloud or alphabet bingo, for example.

Literacy circles are at the heart of Double Oaks' curriculum, which emphasizes listening, speaking, pre-reading and pre-writing skills. Each week's activities are structured around a certain theme. For instance, in a unit devoted to animal habitats, Griggs read the students books about animals and where they live. She also made animal hats for the children to wear in the "playing house" activity center. In the writing center, the names of animals were set out for the students to copy. At the end of the week, Griggs made "worm habitats" (chocolate cupcakes with gummi worms stuck in the center) for a snack.

The students' highly structured day also includes breaks for breakfast and lunch, rest and recess, and work at activity centers. Twice a day, students can circulate among the various centers. Students have a good deal of freedom to choose which activity centers to visit. For instance, at the writing center, students can practice their writing skills by choosing which word cards they want to copy. Children can let their imaginations run free in the "playing house" area, which is complete with stuffed animals, pint-sized furniture and play appliances. But to balance things out, Griggs makes sure each student visits the writing, art, science and math centers at least once a week.

Griggs is aided by a teacher's assistant, Tonya Cunningham. All classrooms at Double Oaks have both a teacher and a teacher's assistant, and students follow the same literacy-based curriculum. Double Oaks also employs a host of other people at the center. A literacy facilitator serves as a resource for the teachers, and also collects and evaluates classroom materials. A social worker is assigned to link the school with the community. A parent advocate and three parent-educator facilitators visit the homes of students to work with their younger siblings, in effect extending Double Oaks' influence to children from infancy on up, to help families make a smooth transition when children start school at Double Oaks.

But academics are only part of the picture at Double Oaks. Socialization is also important. Children learn how to stand in line, share and follow a daily schedule. Basic things, yes, but also essential skills to have in school — and in life.

It's in the social arena, Griggs says, where Javonté has made the most progress since the beginning of the school year. "His social skills are incredible," she says in March. "He got here [in August] and he was shy, into himself. He didn't really interact with the children as well as he does now." One thing Javonté has learned, Griggs says, is to control his temper and be better at sharing and compromising. "His way at first was, 'Leave me alone!' and to push kids away," she says. And, if things didn't go his way, Javonté would sit angrily with crossed arms, or even throw himself on the floor in a fit of temper.

"It was a daily struggle with him getting mad," Griggs says. Now, Griggs says, Javonté still gets upset, but his outbursts are far less frequent. "It can get to the point where a week goes by and we don't have to say anything," she says.

Javonté's growing maturity is clearly recounted in a portfolio of his work. Sometimes, Griggs has the children draw pictures and explain to her what they have created. Based on what the children tell her, Griggs then writes a caption underneath the picture. One of Javonté's pictures shows three smiling figures drawn in red crayon. The caption underneath reads, "I share with my friends." Another crayon drawing carries the caption, "I share my scissors with Nicolas and Marrick."

Javonté's attitudes are also evident in his actions. One Friday afternoon in March, Javonté was at the computer center when Griggs asked him to come outside and help clean up an artist's easel with some other children. "Somebody can use the computer," he invited his classmates, as he got up to help his teacher.

In Griggs' class, Javonté has also learned to write his name, copy written words, and use the computer. He loves to build things and often creates elaborate structures out of blocks. In whatever he does, Javonté wants to share his work with the rest of the class, Griggs says. "He's just really proud of what he does."

Javonté lives with his great-grandmother, Juanita Truesdale, who has raised him since his birth. Javonté's mother, Quella Truesdale, lives across town with his two-year-old sister, Ranisha Barrinter. As his parent, Javonté's great-grandmother agrees that Javonté has learned a great deal at Double Oaks.

She decided to enroll Javonté in pre-kindergarten out of concern that he might not otherwise be ready for school the following year. "I wouldn't say he was behind, but I didn't think he was up with the other kids," she says.

Now, she's proud that Javonté has learned his colors and numbers, can count and write his name, even read a little and use computers. "It's made a great difference, a really big difference," Truesdale says. Like Griggs, Truesdale also says that attending pre-kindergarten has improved Javonté's behavior — he's more patient, and more willing to share his toys. He's even demonstrated his improved behavior skills with her. One morning as she walked Javonté to school, Truesdale says, she was feeling ill and out of sorts. "He told me to leave my attitude at home," she recalls with a laugh. "I thought that was cute."

And, Javonté is excited about school. "He's ready every morning," his great-grandmother says. "I hope he stays that way the whole 12 years."

All pre-kindergarten students are selected for the program based on educational need. Before the school year begins, potential students go through a verbal screening to assess their awareness of literacy and their readiness for school. Those who struggle with the screening test are prime candidates for what Double Oaks has to offer. "We necessarily choose those that we could make a difference for," says Double Oaks' principal, Cheryl Merritt.

The goal is to make sure these children will be up to speed by the time they're in third grade, which in North Carolina is when students take the first standardized end-of-grade test of their school career. On a more immediate level, Merritt says she hopes by the time students graduate from Double Oaks, they will already be in the swing of school, and will be prepared for success in kindergarten. Javonté will attend Nathaniel Alexander Elementary next year, and his classmates at Double Oaks will graduate into more than a dozen feeder elementary schools in north and west Charlotte. "We have forevermore changed what kindergarten teachers will be expecting," Merritt says.

Rather than worrying that these children will lag behind their kindergarten peers next year, the concern is that pre-kindergarten graduates could actually be bored in school next year because they've already learned so many things. The student folders of pre-kindergarten graduates will be specially marked so that their teachers will know they've been through the program.

Though participation in the pre-kindergarten program is optional, parents who enroll their children must sign an agreement to fulfill specific obligations. Parents are expected to attend an orientation, at least one parent-teacher conference and parent workshops, to volunteer at the school, to be at the bus stop in the morning and afternoon, and to commit to reading to their children daily. Parental involvement, Merritt says, is a crucial component. "What is most beneficial is having those students understand what school is, what school is for, and having those parents involved on a consistent basis. That will make the difference, now and forevermore."

Truesdale takes her involvement with Double Oaks seriously. She walks Javonté to and from school every day and she has never missed a meeting of the Parent's Club, a group that meets monthly to teach life skills programs to parents, and provides educational activities for their children. Truesdale always brings Javonté with her to Parent's Club. Javonté also attends after-school activities every Monday through Thursday. Truesdale expects Javonté to stay involved with Double Oaks' after-school programs when he enters elementary school, and as soon as he's old enough she plans to enroll him at summer camp there. Griggs calls Truesdale one of her most reliable parents, always ready to help out when needed.

In keeping with the Double Oaks focus on literacy, Truesdale has read to her great-grandson every night since he began school — especially from "The Three Little Pigs," his favorite book. "I've found it very exciting, and very satisfying," she says. She notices that Javonté is starting to recognize his letters. "Every time he sees a 'J,' he thinks it's his name," Truesdale says.

Truesdale gives high marks to Javonté's teachers and the other school employees, and she checks in with Griggs regularly to keep abreast of what Javonté is doing. "They've got a real good staff," she says.

While Merritt acknowledges the great accomplishments of her school, she is always looking towards improvement. She notes that, so far, Double Oaks has had only fair success in getting parents involved. "We still have a lot to do," she says, adding that Double Oaks is growing and evolving and that overall, she's very happy with the pre-kindergarten program. "I am terrifically pleased," she says.

Double Oaks offers much more than pre-kindergarten. Through its Family Resource Center, Double Oaks also serves children through after-school, weekend and summer educational programs like Support Our Students, an after-school program for at risk kids. Families can get involved with Double Oaks through the Parent's Club; a twice-a-week evening learning gallery with activities for children and parents; and Parent and Child Education, or PACE, that gives parents of pre-kindergarteners a chance to study for their high school equivalency diploma at Double Oaks while their children attend school. "We are constantly coming up with innovative and creative ways to get the parents involved," says Carlenia Ivory, family community resource supervisor at Double Oaks.

Financial and volunteer support from a number of local agencies, groups and businesses has helped make Double Oaks what it is today. Merritt says the center is still developing, with plans to further overlap student learning with community resources.

Javonté doesn't know all this. For now, he just knows that school is fun, and that he likes learning. For now, that's more than enough for a healthy, happy start. ⌢

# Giving Dreams

## Kay Windsor

≈

*S*oft sobs came from the loft where my five-year-old daughter Elizabeth had been sleeping. She had awakened from a bad dream, and when I soothed her back to sleep by brushing my fingers across her eyelids that night, I began the practice of giving her "good dreams," talking to her about the memories of good times and anticipation of special events she could expect when she would wake in the morning. I told her to think of the trip to the library for the kids' cooking contest, the Berenstain Bears book she could purchase with her allowance on the way home, the yellow daffodils we had planted which were ready to bloom, the color of the blue sky on October afternoons when we went for walks in the woods. She closed her eyes, sighed, and went gently back to sleep. It worked, she told me the next day, she had dreamt such good dreams about the Berenstain Bears and our walk in the woods. So began this

*Kay Windsor has been a teacher of high school journalism for 26 years in the Winston-Salem/Forsyth County Schools and was president of the North Carolina Scholastic Media Advisers Association from 1995–1997.*

ritual I often continued of "giving dreams" when we said prayers together at night, my daughter and I. Dreams, both those lost and those realized in ways not expected, are sometimes the strands of experiences we share, the castles we build in the air but wake to build foundations for.

Elizabeth Anna Windsor was born December 31, 1980, our third child and our only daughter. My husband Mike and I were so sure that she would be another boy that we were truly surprised when she arrived on the last day of the year, a calm and sweet New Year's Eve gift. Matt and Aaron, her two older brothers, loved her and doted on her, teased her and taught her to burp louder than most people would imagine possible for a demure little girl with curly blonde hair and deep blue eyes. Little girls with older brothers soon learn to "take up for themselves," my mother told us.

And Elizabeth did. Though she followed her brothers everywhere she could, sometimes pedaling her Strawberry Shortcake tricycle as fast as she could over the ruts and dips in our long driveway, she also let them know when bounds had been overstepped. Sometimes her brothers even called her bossy. It was Elizabeth, after all, who loudly insisted that everybody buckle up each time we traveled in the car. We lived in a log house we had planned and built at the edge of 50 acres of wooded land, and it seemed that every place we needed to go required a 30-minute drive. With children in three different schools and a mother who was a teacher at a fourth school, there was no shortage of PTA meetings, school programs, athletic practices, science fairs and book fairs. We seemed to spend a good deal of time in cars.

When we went to the woods, like Thoreau, we had wanted to simplify our lives and focus on those parts we thought most important. We planned to live in harmony with the environment around us as much as was possible with our three curious, active children. Taking used newspaper, glass, and aluminum to the recycling station became a twice-a-month errand. Elizabeth and her brothers would share the change they earned for the recycled materials they had sorted and packed. We moved to a house on a small stub street 17 miles across the county when the children were 10, 13 and 16, and it was at Elizabeth's urging that we continued to make the recycling runs even though the small payment for the recycled items had ceased.

It was on this new street that Elizabeth met Brooke Barbour, one of her best friends. Like Thoreau, our family had decided to "return to civilization," and we moved out of our small isolated log house to a house with more room for two teenagers and one almost-teen. Elizabeth was elated about this move; even though she missed our little house in the woods, she loved being in a neighborhood and being able to run down the street to see Brooke. For five years it seemed that the two girls lived partly in one house and partly in the other. Only three houses separated them on our street, and they shared tears, joys, secrets, all the stuff of a good friendship. They even bickered occasionally as sisters might.

Elizabeth and Brooke took dance classes together, went to the beach, sleepovers, church camp and youth fellowship activities together; they held Easter egg hunts for the younger children on the street and babysat for them. By the time they began high school, they had added interests and activities that didn't always include the other. Brooke danced on the drill team, and Elizabeth ran on the cross country team. They each had other close friends, some of them mutual, but they also kept the close friendship they had nurtured.

Together, they had made plans on an October Friday afternoon to go to a birthday party just before the football game between West Forsyth, their high school, and R.J. Reynolds, the high school where I teach. I had picked them up after school at West and half-listened as Elizabeth talked on the

phone to four or five friends, sharing plans for the game and
the weekend. Her to-do list, color coded on the dry erase board
in her bedroom, reminded her to get more sponsors for the
6.3 mile CROP walk for hunger on Sunday for youth fellowship, her service club at school and the cross country team.
She towered over me as I worked at the dining room table,
her 5'9" lean frame arched gently as she leaned down to give
me a kiss, a hug and an "I love you." Then she ran out the
door and into the waiting car in our driveway. I stood up and
watched her buckle her seat belt before they drove away.

Elizabeth was killed instantly in a one-car crash less than
a mile from our home on that afternoon, October 11, 1996,
two months before her sixteenth birthday. The driver was a
16-year-old who had received his license a little less than two
months before. Brooke, the front seat passenger, survived, and
is still recovering from traumatic brain injury; the driver
wasn't physically injured. Their destination had been a friend's
house less than five miles away near their high school, then
to the football game across the street. Because the driver had
been driving such a short time, the girls had only recently
been allowed to ride with him and only for short distances
during daylight. (Elizabeth's father, who attended all the football games, had planned to bring Elizabeth and another friend
home after the game.)

Instead, just as my husband was ready to leave to go to
the game, a sheriff's deputy drove into our driveway and gave
us the news that shattered our hearts: a single-car crash.
Massive head injury. Killed instantly. I had heard the sirens
a few minutes earlier and felt vaguely uneasy. Mike, my husband, had passed by the wrecked vehicle a few minutes before; he had almost stopped to offer help, but decided to come
home instead. Emergency vehicles were already there. The
car had traveled off the road and as it started to flip, it had

hit a tree and traveled so far into the brush that my husband could not see it clearly. Elizabeth was buckled into the back seat on the side which hit the tree.

Elizabeth had been driving with a learner's permit the Sunday before she died when I made her let the wheel of the car go off the road onto the soft shoulder. I wanted her to understand how it felt to ease the car back onto the road in that situation. I remembered the surprise I had felt as a new driver losing control of the car when I let the car's wheel slip off the road, jerked it suddenly to return it to the road and lost control. I wasn't hurt, and there was negligible damage to the old tank of a car I drove, but I suddenly knew that I was not invulnerable. Neither driver's education class nor the few hours behind the wheel during in-car training had prepared me for the feeling of helplessness I had when the car wouldn't do my bidding. I wanted Elizabeth to understand that feeling without getting hurt. I wanted her to practice what to do if she ran off the road and needed to correct the steering.

I already knew some of the statistics about young drivers from helping my students do research for stories in the high school journalism courses I taught. One of every four 16-year-old drivers has a traffic accident, and 40 percent of those accidents causes serious injury or death. Driver error is involved in 82 percent of traffic accidents by 16-year-olds. The Centers for Disease Control and Prevention reports that car crashes are still the top killer of youths between 15 and 20.

Now, as I read the numbers which represent fatal crashes in 1996, those figures take on a terrible significance. Of the 41,907 deaths from car crashes in this country in 1996, of the 1,493 lives taken in North Carolina crashes that year, my daughter's was one. Of the 329 15-year-old passengers in fatal crashes in 1996 in the U.S., Elizabeth Anna Windsor was one. Of the five people in our family, of the three children, Elizabeth Anna Windsor was one, is one.

I was a passive advocate of the graduated drivers license proposal before the car crash, but afterward, as I mourned the lost dreams of my daughter, I wrote and called state legislators in support of the proposed graduated drivers license law. I knew, of course, that passage of a graduated drivers license law could not bring my daughter back. I knew that had the GDL law been in effect, it might have made a difference in my daughter's situation. Somehow, I felt, Elizabeth's dreams still needed some validation.

Elizabeth had planned to apply to the School of Design at North Carolina State University. The art portfolio she began is unfinished. Instead of her latest creations, I have 16 portraits of her done by members of her high school art class when she was a model for them the week before she was killed. But, I don't have Elizabeth to hug, to laugh with, to love.

Because I advise a high school newspaper and am active in the North Carolina Scholastic Media Association, I was surrounded by North Carolina high school students who felt that their driving privileges were being unfairly infringed upon with the GDL legislation. NCSMA invited Rob Foss from the UNC Highway Safety Research Center to hold a press conference with the 400 student journalists who attended the North Carolina Scholastic Media Institute last June in Chapel Hill. He armed students with pages of information and gave them a chance to ask questions. Foss, who had studied graduated drivers license policies for several years, dispelled myths about the new legislation for the students.

Since then, students from high school newspapers across the state have written about the graduated drivers license law; I have been surprised that some of them, and some of my own students, have written eloquently about the benefits of the new legislation instead of railing against the loss of "privilege." The new law which went into effect on December 1, 1997, should reduce crash rates by providing new drivers with more experience under safer conditions before allowing them to drive completely on their own. Driving may not be so much the sink-or-swim situation it was before GDL. We won't be throwing nonswimmers into a pool and expecting them to swim just because they have good reflexes and they are young and strong. The 18-month process is designed to protect new drivers (and passengers), not to punish them.

New drivers gain driving privileges in steps as they demonstrate both competence and responsibility. A learner's permit is needed for a year of driving with adult driver supervision before the limited provisional license is obtained. At 15, a young driver can obtain a learner's permit, and if he or she has no violations for a year, the driver may drive alone between 5 a.m. and 9 p.m. with a limited provisional license at age 16. Unsupervised driving late at night is not allowed except for travel to work, for the first six months. The last step of the process, full driving privileges, may be gained if teen drivers have driven safely without violations all this time. All passengers, not just front seat ones, must wear seat belts. (Elizabeth, the self-appointed seat belt militia, would especially approve of that part.)

A student who is affected by the new law wrote in the Ragsdale High School newspaper that "A graduated drivers license procedure is well worth the six months' wait that affords a still-learning driver more experience, practice, and general knowledge about driving and all the responsibilities that go with it."

Some of my own students in journalism classes tackled the subject gingerly, not sure they could argue so strongly against the new law when someone close to them had died. In North Carolina, the National Institute for Citizen Education in the Law found that when students became aware of the numbers of their peers dying in car crashes, they almost unanimously favored the concept of graduated drivers licensing systems. Several of my students who already had permits or licenses on December 1 were supporters at least in part because they were not affected by the law's restrictions, but nearly all of the students, whether they were in favor of the law or not, looked at the statistics with a different view, knowing that at least one of those numbers had been someone they knew, someone their age who did not survive a car crash.

A few hours after the car crash which killed Elizabeth, my husband and I received a phone call from Carolina LifeCare asking about donation of some of Elizabeth's organs and tissue. There was little discussion needed before saying "yes" to the request. Elizabeth had decided when she got her learner's permit during the summer before that she wanted to be an organ donor and had her choice witnessed and labeled on the permit. The little girl who had been our ardent recycler told me she wanted to donate her organs when she died, that after all, that would be the "ultimate recycling." Why not reuse something she wouldn't be needing anymore? she asked. Because she died before arriving at the hospital or being placed on life support, the organs available for donation were the corneas and heart valves. Two people received a cornea each, and two people received heart valves from Elizabeth. I like to imagine that those people have a chance to see some of the beauty around them that Elizabeth held so precious, those blue skies she was always dreaming of and running under. Perhaps the heart valve recipients can even run again, as Elizabeth ran freely under those skies and on her cross country team. I hope that they may have been given some dreams again.

As I write this, during the second Lent since Elizabeth's death, there are a few pink blossoms on the Kwanzan cherry tree we planted in the back yard for her, a gift from friends. I have been to Laurel Ridge with Elizabeth's friends from our New Philadelphia Moravian Church youth group, and Hollie

and Charity showed me the Eastern overlook, Elizabeth's favorite place on those mountains. North Carolina Scholastic Media Association is offering a scholarship to its summer institute in her memory for the second year. The deep blue irises she and I planted together next to the back porch will bloom again soon. The 10 dogwoods her brother planted for her have buds. There have been some blue skies this week, but none to rival the ones we used to see on October walks.

Elizabeth's brother, Aaron, read from Walt Whitman's "Leaves of Grass" at her funeral: "the smallest sprout shows there is really no death." Matt, her oldest brother, read from Dayton Edmonds' "The Circle Again: Birth and Death":

I am a thousand winds that blow.
I am the diamond glint on snow.
I am the sunlight on ripened grain.
I am the gentle autumn rain.
When you awaken in the morning's hush,
I am the swift uplifting rush
Of quiet birds in circled flight.
I am the soft stars that shine at night.
Do not stand at my grave and cry
I am not there, I did not die.

Those lines offer hope and some comfort. I imagine touching my fingers lightly to her eyelids once more to "give dreams" of some of those images. I miss so much Lizzie's exuberant hugs, just because she was happy to be alive, her infectious laughter when she and her Dad mugged at each other in secret conversation, the silly swish of her long blonde hair as she imitated the cheerleaders on "Saturday Night Live," the healthy flush on her face after a three-mile run, those deep blue eyes somewhere between the color of the October sky and the irises we planted. And I miss "giving her dreams" as we said prayers together at the end of the day. ☞

*My husband Mike and I are the parents of three children: Matt (23) a recent graduate of North Carolina State University and a park ranger at Hanging Rock State Park in Danbury, N.C.; Aaron (20) a student at North Carolina State University majoring in computer science; and Elizabeth who was a sophomore at West Forsyth High School when she died October 11, 1996. Being the parents of Matt, Aaron and Elizabeth has been our greatest joy.*

# GENESIS: The Coming into Being

**H e l e n e  C .  K n i g h t**

⌒⌒

J ust as the word defines the creation of the world, so it describes a program aimed to negate the pressures and influences swirling about adolescent boys and to foster the emergence of true, strong manhood.

Targeting African American boys between the ages of 10 and 17 who are struggling to make sense of their chaotic world, this special program has been the beginning for over 200 young men in Gates County. Nestled in the northeastern corner of North Carolina, Gates has less than 10,000 residents. But a disproportionate number of them are youths finding their way into adulthood in a confusing and difficult world.

*Helene C. Knight, a Gates County native, is news editor with the* Gates County Index, *a Media General Inc. subsidiary. A 16-year veteran of print journalism, Knight is actively involved in promoting youth programs within her county. The newspaper has often supported programs such as GENESIS by highlighting its positive aspects. The GENESIS program has been an inspiration for many of the county's African American youth and has produced young men who have made themselves and the group proud.*

When it seems all others wouldn't listen and didn't care, many of these young people growing into adulthood say GENESIS is their only "place of peace" and "haven of hope."

One of those young men, Brandon Holloman, says he doesn't know where he would have ended up without this program. A bright, charismatic young man who stands 5'9" tall in his jeans and t-shirt, Brandon speaks earnestly about GENESIS and its gains. Brandon is the first to tell you his participation has meant a 180-degree turn in his attitude and behavior.

"I was just like most kids, bored and looking for something to do," Brandon explains with a smile. "I wasn't a real bad kid, but I know that there were problems and I honestly didn't know what I needed."

Trouble has a way of attaching itself to 14-year-olds like Brandon, as they navigate through destructive influences like peer pressure, drugs and violence. These influences have trapped young people like Brandon, and for some it has been their downfall.

"I had some problems myself," says Brandon, who bravely pulled himself above the fray of his life with tools he learned from GENESIS. "There were some problems at home, problems at school and some real bad attitude problems, but GENESIS has shown me that attitude is a state of mind and I have to take control of my life."

GENESIS helped Brandon see his own behavior clearly, and how it could pull him off track.

"I was one of those who would 'jump the gun' so to speak at the first sign of trouble. But I know now that that's not the way to be and that I will never accomplish anything unless I set some goals and reach for them," he says with a fresh smile that lights up his face as well as his future.

"I can do anything and be anything I want to be. I just need to make up my mind and concentrate on those positive things."

GENESIS, an educational leadership program which aims to develop independence and strength in young African American men, was founded in Gates County in 1994 and provides a variety of workshops on African American culture, careers, health, life skills and community service. The young men hear talks from motivational speakers and participate in a variety of field trips.

The program broadens many young worlds. "We do so many good things. I've been places I would have never gone if I were not involved in GENESIS," Brandon says.

Brandon is just one of many whose success stories evolve through the program. With a twinkle in his eye and a smile on his young face, Holloman takes the lead in preparing for the group's monthly meeting. He sets up the meeting place workstation and consults with program associate Edward Murphy on what Murphy needs him to do.

Brandon approaches these activities with pride. He stands tall and moves with an air of solid confidence and determination to do things right.

"Now it's important that I be proud of myself and always do my best," he explains later.

When he joined GENESIS, Brandon was timid and anxious. His biggest fear was meeting people and not knowing what they would be like. That has changed in the two years Brandon has been in GENESIS. Brandon is now a confident freshman at Gates County High School. He's more outgoing and always willing to lend a helping hand. "I want to give something back," he says. "One of the parts of the program involves community service projects. You feel so good when you can give something back."

GENESIS surprised Brandon, and in turn, Brandon surprised himself. "I thought it was going to be another one of those boring programs that you hear about, but I was surprised. As time went on, I learned a lot of things I didn't know and I learned to respect people and myself. When I first got involved in the program I had to learn how to control myself. This program has been great. We learn stuff, but we have fun too," he says. "We get to be with kids our own age and we get to help others."

Now more at ease with the program, Brandon continues to absorb the benefits but with less hesitation, more open enthusiasm, and new self awareness.

"I knew I had a problem with controlling my anger and I'm not really sure why. I was what they called 'quick tempered,' but Mr. Murphy taught me that there was no sense in that. He told me instead of being hot tempered, I needed to focus some of that attention on my grades."

This awareness has only fueled his determination to meet goals he has set for himself. "Now I'm trying to do good in school and better myself. I'm trying my best to get on the honor roll before I get out of the ninth grade and I'm going to do it, too. I know I can do it."

Aside from the motivational aspect of GENESIS, Brandon also credits the program with practical matters like helping him learn better study habits. It has also given him a safe and trusted group with which to share his everyday concerns.

"We have our group meetings, but we also take time out to talk about school and schoolwork and our concerns with schools," Brandon says. "GENESIS is a way for us guys to talk about everything. Mr. Murphy just lets us talk sometimes and he sits back and listens."

Brandon appreciates that GENESIS is not just talk, that it's also learning through doing. For the past two years, Brandon and other young men in the program have participated in the county's 4-H program. Each GENESIS member took part in demonstration projects last year. Brandon's presentation on chicken barbecue won a district level award and placed fourth at the state level. "I know this year I'll have to improve on my presentation to make it to the state level again," he says, shining with pride and determination.

Brandon comes from a single-parent home. He is guided by his mother, Cynthia Holloman, and his grandmother, Lois Beamon.

"My mom helps me a lot with my reading and math. She's really good at that," he says. And then Brandon rushes to acknowledge the grace of his grandmother in his life. "She loves to cook a lot," he says. "And I really enjoy her cooking too."

His family inspires him to succeed, and GENESIS helps him translate that desire into practical determination. Brandon looks to his future after speaking of his mother and grandmother. "I just want to make them proud," he says. His new found enthusiasm is a welcome sight for his family. "I want to do well and I'm trying my best now to do that."

Brandon's leadership skills and apparent responsibility have earned him participation in another phase of GENESIS called PEP (Peers Empowering Peers). This branch of the group has older youth working directly with some of the younger children and others in the after-school programs across the county. He tackles PEP with all the enthusiasm he has for GENESIS.

"We go around and get the youth involved in positive things," he explains of his work in the program. "We also spend time with them and help them with homework and other activities. I really enjoy the PEP group meetings because it helps me realize just how far I've come and that I too can help somebody get on the right track.

"PEP for me was like graduation. I know that I've reached one step and I'm proud that someone has the confidence in me to see that I have something to share with someone else. I may be 14, but I can share and help someone, too. That makes me feel really good."

Though young in age, Brandon speaks like a man well into his years. He has been involved in a lot of activities, which he would not have experienced had he not been involved in GENESIS.

GENESIS started with a $30,000 grant from the Z. Smith Reynolds Foundation to the NC Cooperative Extension Service, Gates County Center. It has molded a great number of youth and responsible young men who have a more directed future. Like Brandon, they are strong enough to voice appreciation. Independence, after all, needs a strong foundation, a foundation GENESIS gives them.

"I don't know what I would have done without my mother and Mr. Murphy. They have both been good to me. Mr. Murphy is really keeping his eyes on me and has been a good role model. He's showed me a lot and got me on the right track. I really appreciate that and will forever be in his debt."

But Brandon knows the bonds of GENESIS go beyond just a program.

"GENESIS is like family. Everybody can talk and get along. We all kid each other and even say bad things to one another sometimes, but really we all know that we got each other's back and we'll be there when the other one needs help," says Brandon.

Brandon has also learned not to be embarrassed or apologize for the good things he enjoys. And he's not timid about explaining them. Like most 14-year-olds, Brandon enjoys basketball, football and Nintendo. But he also enjoys spending time with his younger cousin and just being with family. "Sometimes you get a lot of talk from the kids because you like to be around your family and stay close to home," Brandon says. "But I don't care what they say, I'm not trying to be something because that's what they expect me to be. I want to be my own person and do the right thing." ⌒

# Being A Parent

## Knight Chamberlain

⥤⥢

Being a parent in the nineties is a constantly evolving challenge. The so-called "traditional family" where the husband works outside the home and the wife works inside the home no longer applies. Today there are two-income households, single-parent households, even same-sex households. Each household is faced with its own set of challenges when it comes to raising happy, productive, well-adjusted children.

It is important, if not imperative, then, that parents not get trapped into traditional courses of action where child raising is concerned. Sometimes it takes imagination. Sometimes it takes common sense. Sometimes it takes a willingness to challenge the status quo, consider possibilities and throw assumptions out the window.

*Knight Chamberlain, a native North Carolinian, is editor of* The News-Journal *in Raeford. He enjoys reading, playing guitar, photography and coaching youth soccer. He freelances for* The News & Observer *(Raleigh)*, The Atlanta Journal-Constitution, The New York Times *and* Washington Post.

My wife, Sandy, and I have three children: Shane, who is now 21 and an artist; Christen, who is 16 and a poet; and Kevin, who is 10 and a writer like his old man. I describe them this way to make a point. Parents generally describe their children in terms of their schooling. That's the way it's always been, but there is nothing that says you have to do it that way.

Raising children is a series of memorable moments woven into the tapestry of their lives. Parents need to recognize that they control whether those memories are pleasant or painful.

I started eating lunch at school with all three of my children when they were in grade school. To this day I'm not sure why. My parents never did it. I didn't know anyone else who did it. It may have been because I worked at a day care center two days a week while I was in college. I saw such delight on the childrens' faces one day when their parents came by to eat biscuits with butter the kids had churned from cream that morning. It was clearly a memorable moment in their lives and my kids still talk about how much they enjoyed my coming by to have lunch with them.

I'm not sure I fully appreciated why I enjoyed it so much until I read something by Benjamin Stein, who once wrote speeches for President Richard Nixon. Stein talked about parents who are too obsessed with their careers to spend time with their children, observing that it was not just bad for the kids, but also a waste for the parents.

He recognized that children can be a bottomless well of love and esteem if their parents make even the tiniest effort to tap into them. To the rest of the world you're just a worker; to your kids you can be an idol. If you work hard, you can usually make enough money to put bread on the table and keep a roof over your head. If you don't get promoted this month, there's always another chance. But the few years between five and 15, when your child is articulate, insightful and boundlessly affectionate, go by incredibly fast.

For those few minutes in the school cafeteria the kids had my undivided time and attention. I wasn't rushing to get them out the door to school or rushing to get them home from school or busy watching the television or reading the paper or fixing supper. I was all theirs, and they loved it. And that's only one example.

This whole process began before I even officially became a father.

Sandy had Shane by a previous marriage. He was three when we met, so seat-of-the-pants fatherhood became an evolving process. At the time I was the sports writer for a community newspaper. I thought taking Shane with me to cover a high school baseball game sounded like a good idea. I had no idea what I was getting myself into. When he started running all over the place, I wondered if I'd made a mistake. Instead it marked the beginning of a somewhat unorthodox element of child rearing.

As the years went by I worked different jobs with one common denominator — they all had flexible hours involving evenings and weekends. Coincidentally, Sandy's schedule as a nurse was rigid and unbending, all involving evenings and weekends. We had no family close by and we couldn't afford a sitter. End result. Where I went, the kids usually followed.

Before Shane started school, I was the Continuing Education Coordinator in Scotland County for Richmond Community College. That meant traveling to different places and towns in the county to register classes, deliver books and equipment, and sometimes collect money. Shane quickly became my administrative assistant and quite popular with the teachers and students alike. On those occasions when he wasn't motivated to come along, the promise of a small toy or trip to McDonald's generally did the trick. Lest anyone believe such an arrangement was paving the way for juvenile blackmail, i.e., "I won't go unless you do this," I was careful to follow through on every promise.

This kind of small detail manifested benefits in unexpected ways. This attention at an early age builds and maintains self-confidence through the years. It is well documented that a high percentage of children enter kindergarten with a positive self-image, then that percentage plummets by the time they reach high school.

As Shane got older, Sandy and I adopted some ideas we'd picked up from magazines. Others we made up on our own. Once, when his grades were suffering while he was in the seventh grade and he wasn't doing his homework, we told Shane, fine, you don't like school, you don't have to go anymore. Just stay home and watch TV. He was visibly shaken by the offer, he never tried it and we never had to suggest it again. Unorthodox, but effective. We probably wouldn't try this approach with our other children, but knowing Shane through the close relationship we had developed over the years, I felt confident that this would work. Thankfully, it did.

We also made a point to love the child, improve the behavior. We made a pact with Shane that if he ever got in trouble, he could tell us about it right away and we would honor a 24-hour cooling off period with no yelling or lectures. We also chose our battles. When he dyed his hair black and asked to get his ear pierced, we decided that was something we could live with. It paled in comparison to drugs and alcohol by a mile.

Our patience and faith in these methods were severely tested, however, when Shane dropped out of high school only four months before graduation. His grandmother, with whom he was very close, had died after a long battle with cancer, leaving him despondent and miserable. He drifted from one job to another, and even left home to live with some friends in a trailer with no heat, no hot water and no telephone. We fought the urge to intervene, convinced that the seeds we'd planted would bear fruit.

Sure enough, he finally came home and said he understood what we had been trying to tell him. Like the prodigal son, we welcomed him back, the past forgotten. He finished high school at the community college and enrolled at the University of North Carolina at Pembroke from which he will graduate with a solid education.

Christen also made the rounds with me at work. At first she slept in baby carrier. Later I carried a sleeping pad, pillow and blanket in the car for her. When she got old enough, she too became my administrative assistant and occasional navigator on road trips. She was an effective icebreaker on interviews and became a fixture with the cheerleaders when I covered football and basketball games.

She remembered going to work with me and my letting her try and type on the computers or typewriters, whichever I happened to have. She remembered trying to write stories like her daddy and selling newspapers. She remembered going to work with me every morning and going to get hot chocolate before school. She remembered that I always wanted to eat lunch with her on the days the school served vegetable soup and a peanut butter and jelly sandwich because I liked it so much.

When Kevin was a baby I bought a carrier that enabled me to carry him on my back. That way I could take him to basketball or football games, take notes and shoot pictures while he just watched everything going on around him and took it in. He traveled with me all over the state, as did Shane and Christen. An unexpected benefit of all this is that all three have learned to travel long distances well, either sleeping, reading or engaging us in conversation. This makes for much more pleasant vacationing experiences rarely marred by whining and complaints and the endless calls of Are we there yet? and, How much longer?

Each child had a pet name. It also brought us closer in conversation. We were partners on the road. For a while, Kevin and I had a little routine going where I would call him "my buddy." He would respond "my big buddy." I would come back with "my little buddy." Then we would go back and forth: "my soccer buddy," during soccer season, "my sleepy buddy" at bedtime and so forth.

We always had a king size bed and it wasn't unusual for all five of us to be in it for at least a little while before bedtime. Sandy and I used to complain about how the kids always seemed to have to be around us, but we really weren't complaining. We wanted them there and they wanted to be with us. Even today Shane kisses his mother goodbye, Christen calls us at least once a day from school, and Kevin, our 10-year-old "tough guy" who plays several sports and watches pro wrestling, still kisses me goodbye when I drop him off at school, comes up and hugs us "just because," and occasionally falls asleep in our bed cupping one of our hands in each of his. These "little things" nurtured and encouraged through the years have created inseparable bonds.

Through the years we have recognized their achievements with token financial rewards and with impromptu celebrations. Whenever possible we attend their school open houses and teacher conferences, their recreational soccer, baseball and basketball games, and their musical performances. When they ask us questions we try to answer them or encourage them to seek the answers on their own. We encourage them to try new things, challenge their abilities and stretch their imaginations. We tell them they can do anything they set their minds to.

It isn't a matter of trying to create super kids or child geniuses. We never tell them they have to make straight A's or that they will become doctors or lawyers when they grow up. We don't make them study five hours a day or practice seven days a week. We want them to be children as long as they can and believe that time, experience and maturity will take care of the rest.

Spending time with them and getting to know them as individuals helped us learn how to deal with them on an individual basis.

When Shane told us he wanted to major in art in college, the announcement didn't land on us like a ton of bricks. We knew he had the talent, but we also know he has practical skills he can fall back on to support himself financially as he pursues his dream.

We recognized that Christen has a lot of drive, a strong work ethic, and a need to be challenged. When she was in the eighth grade I started talking to her about the School of Science and Math in Durham. I read the student profiles and realized she fit the school like a glove. Christen wasn't so sure, but I knew she tended toward self-doubt and needed encouragement and prodding. There was never a doubt in my mind that she would make it, but I conveyed that confidence in a way that worked. It's a game we play. I know she believes in herself, but she needs the affirmation from me.

To that end I would like to share this final story.

Those of you who are college basketball fans likely enjoyed the drama played out in Oklahoma City where Valparaiso's Bryce Drew put up a miracle three-point shot at the buzzer to upset Mississippi in the first round of the NCAA basketball tournament last March. The embrace between Drew and his father-coach, Homer, after the game spoke volumes about their relationship.

I was blessed with a similar experience last summer which

I mention, not to brag, but to illustrate the power of positive reinforcement.

Kevin was playing in the city minor league baseball championship game between the Pirates and the Rangers. He had a great game, slamming a triple and then stealing home for what looked like a commanding 10–3 lead.

But the Rangers made a comeback, and in the bottom of the last inning the score was 10–7 with one out and the bases loaded. That's when Kevin was called to the mound to finish the inning.

It was the best of times, it was the worst of times. Suddenly I understood what that quotation was all about. I was elated that the coach had so much confidence in Kevin, but I was anxious at the same time. It was one of those watershed moments when you realize you can no longer shield your child from that which can cause him pain and disappointment. I looked over at Sandy. "I can't look," she said, covering her eyes. "That's my baby."

Kevin took his warm-up pitches and finally the umpire shouted "play ball" and motioned the batter into the box. Calls of encouragement rose up from both sides.

Kevin went through his wind-up and let the ball fly. "Crack," the batter lifted a hit over first base and scored the kid from third. The bases were still loaded and now the score was 10–8. It didn't look good, but I was relieved that Kevin didn't appear all that concerned about it.

The next batter stepped up. The cheers from both sides got louder. Kevin wound up again. Foul Ball! He pitched again. Strike two! He pitched again. Strike three! Two outs, one to go.

Now both sides were on their feet. The tension had built to the pressure-cooker level. Kevin wound up again. A swing and a miss. The infielders were punching the sky with their fists and the outfielders were jumping up and down exhorting Kevin to "do it again."

Then it happened. A Hollywood script writer couldn't have sketched it out any better. Kevin's next pitch went into the dirt and scudded past the catcher. The third base coach waved his runner to steal home. Kevin took off for home to cut off the runner. The catcher found the ball and fired it to Kevin. Kevin caught the ball, lost his footing and slid past home plate, but not before tagging out the sliding runner for the final out. Game over, Pirates win!

I started breathing again and watched the coaches and players mob Kevin and each other in celebration. Later, after everyone gathered for the team championship picture, I knelt down and gave Kevin a hug.

"Weren't you nervous when that kid hit your first pitch?" I asked him, remembering how calm he'd seemed under the circumstances.

"Well, not really," he said with a shrug of his shoulders. "You and Mom always tell me I can do anything if I try hard enough."

It was one of those moments that lasts a lifetime and it reinforced everything I have learned about raising a happy, well-adjusted, confident child.

All kids experience a progression of successes and failures growing up. The ones whose parents (or parent, or guardian) pick them up, reassure them and encourage them when they fall will gain the confidence to try again. In the process they learn that life's setbacks are really just stepping stones to success. But really knowing your child is the difference be-tween offering tired platitudes versus genuine support and encouragement.

That's why Drew and his father hugged the same way af-ter Valparaiso was knocked out of the championship hunt. Win or lose, you love your children just the same. ⪧

# Growing Up Fast

## Elizabeth Warren

≈⊃⊂

eisha and I met for the first time when her baby, Rayshawn, was two-and-a-half months old. Tammy, a social worker with the Exchange Club Center, took me to Keisha's house in Raleigh one hot and humid August day in 1997 to get acquainted, and to help Keisha set goals as a participant in the Adolescent Parenting Program.

Keisha seemed shy. She didn't say much, but she smiled often, showing beautiful dimples. Her goals were ambitious: stay out of the wrong crowd, make friends with other teens in the program, set up day care for Rayshawn, get a monthly Depo-provera birth control shot, go to scheduled doctors' ap-

*Elizabeth Warren is the Director of Communications at Prevent Child Abuse North Carolina. She serves as Keisha's mentor through the Adolescent Parenting Program conducted by the Exchange Club CAP Center of Wake County. The goals of the program include postponing a second pregnancy, staying in school, and learning positive parenting skills. Elizabeth completed a 12-hour volunteer training last summer and began working with her teen in September of 1997. Volunteers meet weekly with their teen for at least a year.*

pointments. . . . As the list continued, I recognized some of the same goals I struggle with: get eight hours of sleep a night, follow an exercise plan (walk and do sit-ups), and read books on parenting.

I asked to hold the baby soon after we arrived, and Keisha handed him over without qualms. Rayshawn had a head full of glossy curls and smiled at me enthusiastically. He was alert, responsive, and neat as a pin, despite the August heat. I was surprised at how tired my arm got holding the baby as we talked, and I was a little relieved when Keisha took Rayshawn back onto her lap. I was not used to holding a baby, and the magnitude of having a child at Keisha's age rested on me.

Keisha impressed me that first day with how calmly and confidently she interacted with her son. Throughout our relationship, I have continued to marvel at how strong and accomplished she is despite the swirl of poverty and violence that surround her. She has shared her story with me in the hope of helping other teenage girls.

Keisha got pregnant when she was 15. It "just happened," she says quietly, almost resignedly. She hadn't wanted a baby and says that Rayshawn was conceived on the one occasion she didn't use birth control. She knew about how babies were made from sex education classes taught at school, and she had also talked to her cousin and one of her older sisters about sex.

Keisha knew that she was pregnant when she woke up one morning and went in the kitchen to drink some tea.

"I kept gagging and felt like I was going to throw up," she remembers. "And then I knew. I didn't tell Daddy and them, but I had bought some tampons that I didn't use. I meant to take some out like I was using them, but I forgot." Her father noticed and confronted her. He was mad at first and "fussed" at her. But her father was not angry with Keisha's boyfriend, who is six years Keisha's senior, because, Keisha says, "we went out together about three-and-a-half months" — a long time in a teenager's life.

Keisha's father's girlfriend, Debbie, who lives with them, took Keisha to the doctor for prenatal care. Debbie has a daughter of her own who was a teen mom at a younger age than Keisha, so she was accepting of the situation.

At first Keisha was unhappy about the pregnancy. "I felt like I was the only young person who ever got pregnant, and I was embarrassed to be around my family because I was so young," she says. "I was embarrassed even though my cousin had her first baby at 13 and her second at 15." While no one in Keisha's extended family said anything negative directly to her, one cousin told her that some of them had been talking about her. They were saying that they knew she would get pregnant, because she was "fast" and "trying to be grown."

The truth is that Keisha was somewhat reluctant to have sex. Jay, the father of Keisha's baby, put pressure on her. "He kept asking me when we was going to get up and stuff," she says. "In a way I just wanted to do it 'cause all my friends were doing it. Everybody was just having it, so I thought it was fun."

Keisha didn't tell Jay when she learned she was pregnant. She and Jay had broken up. She thinks her father may have told him. But when Keisha saw Jay in a store with his current girlfriend after she began showing, neither he nor Keisha brought up the subject of the baby that was obviously on the way. Later that day he showed up at her house to talk. "He didn't really show any emotion," Keisha says, when she confirmed that the baby was his. He didn't offer to help. Jay lives with his girlfriend and her two children by another man.

Jay's involvement with Rayshawn is limited. He takes the baby for the weekend occasionally, but Keisha says it seems to her that her son always comes back from his dad's with something wrong, like bad diaper rash or the stomach flu. Jay doesn't give her any money for the baby, and he makes promises that he doesn't keep. Recently he said he would take the baby for the weekend and buy him things that he needed. Jay did take Rayshawn, who came back sick, but he didn't shop for him. Keisha has never expected much from Jay. She is mildly irritated rather than angry about his lack of support. "He lies about stuff. You can't count on him," she says.

More helpful is the subsidized day care Keisha receives. To qualify, she had to fill out a statement disclosing her financial resources. Jay wrote on the papers that he contributes $50 a week, which is untrue, and signed his name. Unable to convincingly alter the figure to $0, Keisha changed the amount to $25. Jay's lie means that she must pay a couple of dollars a month for day care, instead of receiving the service for free. A couple of dollars is a large amount of money to Keisha. Her total income per month is $160.

With her $160, Keisha struggles each month to buy diapers, wipes, baby food, clothes, books, toys, and any other baby necessities. Having Medicaid and WIC (Special Supplemental Food Program for Women, Infants and Children) helps, but she still has to borrow money from other people. Recently she borrowed $26 for daycare and other expenses from Debbie. Her grandmother also lends her money sometimes.

While she clearly loves Rayshawn a great deal, Keisha doesn't hesitate to tell other girls who are having sex without birth control of the possible repercussions. Her life as a single, teen-age mom is very difficult. The struggle to improve her situation and Rayshawn's is constant and often overwhelming.

"Being a mom is not what I expected," Keisha warns. "It's not a baby doll. I thought you just had to feed it and put clothes on it and that's it, but it's not. You can't just lay it aside when you get tired. It's best to wait 'till you are married and out of school so you can support yourself and your family so you don't have to depend on other people. You can't count on them."

Keisha's biggest fear about her future is that she won't be able to go to college and get a good job. Keisha doesn't want her son to "live in the projects or in a shack," she says. "I want Rayshawn to be able to have whatever he needs. Also, I was abused physically as a child. I don't want to do that to him."

Keisha's mom abandoned her at birth, and she was raised mostly by her father's mother, who beat her.

"I used to hate her and wish she was dead," Keisha says of the time she was living with her grandmother. "I used to wish that I was born into another family."

As a teenager, Keisha began hitting back and was arrested on assault charges. Although pregnant, she was sent to one of North Carolina's training schools. She reports that she gets along better with her grandmother now that she's older and doesn't live with her. She even chooses to spend time at her grandmother's house when things get rough with her and her dad.

Keisha says that she never hits nine-month-old Rayshawn. But when asked if she will hit him when he's older, she answers honestly that she can't say. Although she knows that hitting is ineffective and wrong, she's uncertain about what she should do instead to control Rayshawn's behavior when he's big. Hitting "didn't work for me," she says. "It only hurt for a little while, and then you go back and do the same old thing."

While often exhausted, Keisha is proud of what she is accomplishing. "I'm still in high school and making good grades, and I'm able to take care of Rayshawn," she says. "Even though I do ask people to borrow money, nobody really keeps him except Jay or Denise [Keisha's best friend] and her mother. Other than that, he's with me." She smiles, showing her dimples.

Keisha likes a lot of things about being a mom. One of her favorite things is watching her baby learn something new. She believes that Rayshawn "is going to be my best friend."

"When I'm upset," she says, "he makes me feel better. Like the other day I was crying about something, and Rayshawn was on the floor playing and grinning at me. I started grinning too." The best things about Rayshawn are that "he likes to play, and he likes to eat. He's always smiling and laughing, and he has a lot of energy."

But parenting is tough, too, she says. "My friends, they be going out on weekends, and I can't go nowhere. I don't want to put him off on other people. I think I grew up too fast. I haven't even gone to the prom yet. I don't think I'm going to have a teen life."

Keisha knows these sacrifices show her strengths. "I'm responsible," she says. "When I get money, I got to take care of business first. He comes first all the time. I'm good at not just throwing him off on anybody, like a lot of young girls. I'm also good at keeping him clean."

Keisha feels that the Adolescent Parenting Program has helped her significantly by both teaching her about parenting and helping out in desperate situations. "It's important to learn about the different topics that we do, like how to handle stress and play with your child," she says. "When you run out of milk, they try to provide it. I love having a volunteer. I like to go places. I like getting out of the house."

The program is structured so that the young moms and their volunteers meet monthly as a group to socialize and learn parenting and life skills such as budgeting, communication, and child development. APP's coordinator often arranges for a speaker, video or game on that month's topic. These monthly meetings are held at the church located next to the Exchange Club CAP Center in the Mordecai section of Raleigh.

In addition to the volunteers and social worker from the APP, Keisha names other people who provide her with support. She says that her neighbor helps occasionally, and she can count on her best friend, Denise, and her mother, Mary. Mary used part of her tax refund to buy Keisha a pair of new tennis shoes and a t-shirt. Keisha's grandmother offers to watch the baby, but, Keisha adds sternly, "I don't want her to hit him. I'm scared to leave him with her." Yet Keisha has never talked with her grandmother about her concerns. "She's not a very easy person to talk to," she explains.

Keisha's dream is to go to college at N.C. State and be an obstetrician or pediatric nurse. She's also interested in being "a nurse like when the baby's born," working with special kids or preemies, or being a correctional officer. "I want to do a lot of stuff. I haven't narrowed it down," she says. Keisha hopes to get a scholarship somewhere and says she has always wanted to live in a dorm. Realistically, she's concerned that having a baby will keep her from going to the prom or living on campus in a dorm room.

Keisha knows that many barriers stand between her and college, and she knows that she won't be able to get a good job without getting an education. Her father is terminally ill, which adds to her family's stress and makes it more difficult for them to get ahead financially, and impossible to pay for school. Their "raggly" duplex, as Keisha describes it, is too small for their family, and the lack of her own space makes studying more difficult. She hopes that they will move to a better place, but she doesn't know when.

Recently, Tammy, Keisha, and I met at her grandmother's house to review her goals at the start of the program and set new ones. It was a warm spring day, sunny and breezy, and we sat on the back porch to talk. Rayshawn can crawl now, even pull up on his two feet, and he says a few words. He smiled his enthusiastic smile (now with teeth!) as he played with my necklace.

While the baby played, we talked about all that Keisha has accomplished since last summer. She has met her most important goals: delaying a second pregnancy, securing child care, attending high school, and learning parenting skills and techniques. Despite her circumstances, Keisha demonstrates exceptional maturity and gives excellent care to her son. Rayshawn is a happy, healthy baby who receives plenty of positive attention from his mom. We helped her set new, more ambitious goals for herself for the next six months.

But despite her strengths, Keisha can only achieve the things that she wants for herself and her son — a good education, a good job, and a decent place to live in a safe neighborhood — if she has support from others. She's really very much like the rest of us.  ⌐

# Seeing
# Them Smile

## Paul    Bonner

≈⌒

A van pulls up outside, and Carol Sanderson looks out the front window of the small cinder block building in Wake Forest that she and her teenage daughter, Christy, call their warehouse. On this overcast Saturday in late January, they're expecting a church youth group from Lumberton, volunteer helpers in the work ahead. This doesn't look like the group, only three teenagers with a woman, none of whom they recognize.

"Who are these people?" Christy asks.

"Go find out," Carol urges.

The newcomers have heard about Christy. They come in the front door carrying bulging garbage bags, past the sign on the wall that reads "Kids Helping Kids."

"I've seen your picture in the paper," Allison Redfern, the woman, says to Christy. She leads the teenagers into the warehouse, where they all set down the bags, which are

*Paul Bonner is a reporter for* The Herald-Sun *and a freelance writer. He lives in Durham with his wife and two sons, Andrew (18) and George (11).*

full of used toys. "They're all clean," Redfern says.

What Christy and Carol Sanderson need right now even more than toys is help packing them into boxes and loading them onto a semi-trailer parked beside the building. That won't be a problem if enough volunteers show up. The next step, however, is far from settled: getting the toys to where they are needed. Carol has spent hours on the phone — much of it very long distance — trying without success to arrange transportation.

Over the past three years, Operation Toy Box, as Christy named the project for which she has become famous, has sent tens of thousands of toys to young disaster victims in the Virgin Islands and to Grand Forks, N.D. This time, Christy is targeting the Pacific island and U.S. territory of Guam, recently battered by a typhoon. It lies nearly 10,000 miles away, more than three times farther than both previous shipments combined. The airlines are sympathetic but, so far, politely noncommittal. The Sandersons have gone ahead and started packing, hoping for a breakthrough.

Soon, the youth group drives up, and Christy puts them to work, first showing them the classification system. Action figures, for example, are sorted mostly by their corresponding animated movies.

"Horses, Hunchback, Toy Story, Anastasia — of course Power Ranger always overflows — Simpsons, Space Jam," Christy says as she leads them through narrow aisles between the homemade shelves. Along one wall are large bins piled high with stuffed animals and dolls whose plush and polyester must be untangled after washing. The youth group's girls and a woman chaperone take to this work with zeal; sitting beside the bins, they will comb and brush with hardly a break most of the day. There are shelves of games, books ("we get tons of books") and puzzles, those with missing pieces relegated to a bottom shelf "because we don't throw anything away."

Christy does throw away a few toys, such as the sword in a green scabbard she spots, snatches from a shelf and drops into a garbage bag.

"We don't do violence," she says. "We just trash it." This prohibition extends to toy guns of all descriptions.

The merely grotesque ones, mostly boys' action figures, aren't necessarily pitched but undergo a kind of quarantine in a large box labeled "weird men." Carol examines a "Hammerhead Shark Street Fighter" still in its package and deposits it there.

As the volunteers fill boxes, Chad Pulley, 21, labels them and puts them on the trailer. The son of an acquaintance of Carol's, he answered her plea one Halloween night to help dig ditches around the warehouse, which was flooding. It still floods regularly, and Chad and Christy have become close friends. He is Operation Toy Box's treasurer.

Then Christy drives the family's van in to Raleigh to make the last toy pickup of what she and her mother have called "Cheer Lift to Guam." As she drives, she talks animatedly about her toy relief work and how it and nationwide attention have made her life as a student at Meredith College in Raleigh a bit unusual. She entered the college as a freshman in fall 1997. Carol works there as an associate director of financial aid.

Christy's love of toys and children has in many ways made her mature beyond her years. The college administration secretary takes phone messages for her. Her dormmates have grown used to the occasional media spotlight, as when a photographer and reporter for *People* magazine visited last fall. Through it all, Christy has worked harder, with longer hours — and, she believes, with greater satisfaction — than she would have at any paying job.

"I'm not used to being able to sit down and take a break," she says. "I don't remember what I did before Operation Toy Box."

She is planning to major in speech communication and business but hasn't had a chance yet to take any upper-level courses. By the time she does, she may be the only student who has formed her own nonprofit corporation. Certainly, she will be the only student who has been invited to speak on the other side of the continent, at a prep school in Nevada, about community service. She already has addressed an informal gathering of Meredith's trustees, one of whom speculated afterward "she could sell ice at the North Pole."

The story of Operation Toy Box's genesis has been recounted in — besides *People* — *The Chicago Tribune*, local news media, and several magazines. It began in September 1995 when Christy and her mother were watching a television news program in the living room of their Wake Forest home. A segment on Hurricane Marilyn's damage to the U.S. Virgin Islands included a few seconds of footage of a boy pushing a toy grocery cart along a muddy path. In the cart was a toy truck. The boy looked at the camera and smiled.

The fleeting image left a vivid impression on mother and daughter, and they talked about it. Why was the boy smiling? Perhaps, they decided, it was because, despite the devastation all around him, he at least still had the belongings that mattered most in his child's thinking: his toys.

Christy understood. She had Charles, the teddy bear to which she'd confided all her troubles from the time she was four, including her parents' divorce. She was 16, but she wasn't too old to still feel an attachment to the toy. She knew what she would do. She would collect good, used toys for the children of the Virgin Islands.

She distributed a letter to the nearly 1,500 students at her school, Wake Forest-Rolesville High School. In it, she told about Charles.

"I cannot imagine a storm coming along and taking him away forever," she wrote. Comparable misfortune, however, had befallen children in the Virgin Islands. Her schoolmates could join her in sending them toys to replace what they had lost.

The toys started coming in and the word spread. Other schools collected toys. The Food Lion chain allowed drop-off sites in its Wake County supermarkets. Soon, 6,000 toys were on their way to the Caribbean, flown there free by USAir.

After seeing the toys off, Christy climbed back into the family van. Her foot felt a soft lump on the floor. It was a stuffed toy dog that somehow had been left behind.

"Mom, we forgot one," Christy said, and held up the dog.

"Christy, we've got 76 boxes on the airplane, and they're already set to go."

"Fine, he'll go next time."

"What do you mean, 'next time?'"

The answer was clear enough once they both found they missed the excitement of a community-wide mission and, for Christy, just the fun of being around a lot of toys.

"I play with all the stuffed animals," she admits. "Well, you have to test it all," she adds, laughing.

One time her high school friends came to help, and they all wound up wearing elephant masks and running around the warehouse, shouting into walkie-talkies. Then they broke out a ring-toss set, threw rings and, giggling helplessly, caught them on their elephant trunks.

When the Red River flowed over its banks and swept through North Dakota and parts of Minnesota in spring 1997, Christy again collected toys, this time sending more than 8,200. The Roadway trucking company shipped them free.

Meanwhile, the national media exposure brought offers of help from as far away as Ohio and Pennsylvania. Christy has received letters containing praise for her efforts and offers of help from people in 41 states and three Canadian provinces.

Christy parks the van in front of the Bobby Murray Chevrolet dealership in Raleigh, nearly the last pickup point for Cheer Lift of about 50 in the Raleigh area. In the show-room, the back of a truck contains with stuffed animals and other toys: a football still in its box, a toy truck, Mr. Potato Head, Barbie, Barney. People have brought them in response to public service messages on a local radio station.

Christy starts stuffing the toys into garbage bags.

"Should we put them in your van?" an employee asks.

"Yeah," Christy says, then adds: "Unless you want to give me one to take them home in." The man just smiles.

She drives to an Eckerd drug store, the very last pickup point.

"This is the store with the nice manager," she says before going in. She peers into the large cardboard box just inside the front door. Inside are several handfuls of action figures, most of them the kind that come in kid's meals at fast-food restaurants — trinket toys, she calls them. The store is across the street from a public housing apartment complex. Christy says the prevalence of the these fast-food artifacts is a barometer of the percentage of the surrounding population below the poverty level.

As she fishes out the toys, the manager, whose name, Nellie Howard, is on a nameplate pinned to her blouse, walks up. She calls Christy "baby" and thanks her.

Collecting toys has given Christy expert knowledge of their quality and kids' preferences. She has learned to tell by squeezing it whether a teddy bear is a "fair bear" — a cheap knockoff given as a prize at a carnival booth and incapable of withstanding machine washing — or one built to survive a child's attentions. She and her mother sometimes joke about the possibility of finding valuable, out-of-production Beanie Babies and selling them for a steep price, although they haven't yet been faced with the temptation. She has pondered the Barney phenomenon.

"Children absolutely adore Barney," she says of public television's purple dinosaur. The affection is not generally shared by parents — or by her.

"You can tell when a parent has gone through a child's toy box, because there's usually a Barney. We could have a bin just for Barneys. You've got talking Barney, you've got singing Barney. I hate Barney."

Back at the warehouse, more volunteers have arrived. Melvin Whisnant troubleshoots the battery-operated toys, trying fresh batteries and taking the toys apart to check connections if they still don't work.

Charles Richardson, a Red Cross volunteer from Raleigh who has recently returned from Guam, is packing toys. When he left the island January 7, 1998, three weeks after the typhoon, the water still wasn't drinkable, much of the island was still without power and people were still living in shelters. The Red Cross provided the shelters, but it didn't have toys for the children in them.

"Toys are great. Children love toys," he says. "Did you ever see a child who didn't welcome a toy?"

In a small office near the front door, Carol Sanderson is musing about her latest attempts to get someone to fly the toys. A public relations man at Continental had said earlier that the airline could perhaps help.

"I said we'll have about 100 boxes, and he took a deep breath and said he'd have to get back to me," she says. "I said, 'There's 9,000 children who lost all of their toys. Of course there's going to be a lot of toys.' He said he'd call on Tuesday. That's Monday, our time."

The organization's treasury has been essentially empty lately, although an unexpected $520 donation has come in a few days earlier.

"It's going to pay the phone bill," Christy says.

"Our phone bills are . . ." Carol pauses to find the right adjective — "scary."

She picks up from a table one of the Kid Kits that they make. These go to victims of smaller disasters right around home — house fires and evacuations. It's a resealable plastic bag containing crayons, scissors, some glue and Operation Toy Box's own coloring book. With each one, Christy includes a stuffed animal. She wants to send a supply of them to all 58 Red Cross chapters in the state.

"We did 400 before we ran out of money," Carol says. "Really, we want to do this nationwide."

Christy got a letter last December from a Red Cross manager

in Morganton who said he gave one to a young boy whose family had been burned out. (After the article appeared in *People*, she also received a personal letter from the Red Cross' national president, North Carolina native Elizabeth Dole.)

"I wish you could have seen the little boy's face when I handed him a stuffed monkey and the crayons, etc., attached," the manager, Henry Rowland wrote. "I hope you have many opportunities to directly see the happiness your program provides. It certainly made my day."

In fact, Christy has enjoyed almost no such opportunities. Her motto is "turning tears into smiles, one child at a time," but on this day in January, she hasn't yet had a chance to see those smiles for herself. During the first collection, the one for the Virgin Islands, a Raleigh organization donated a plane ticket so she could accompany the toys. Instead, she cashed in the ticket to buy more toys.

Finally, the youth group and other volunteers leave for home. As the winter light slowly fades outside, Christy and her mom and Chad keep packing toys and putting them on the trailer. By the end of the weekend it holds 113 boxes containing 9,800 toys.

In the days following, their phone bill gets even scarier while their hope dims of ever getting the toys to Guam. Carol tries another airline, while in Guam, U.S. Representative Robert Underwood (the island has a non-voting member of Congress) says his efforts to ship them through FEMA, the Federal Emergency Management Agency, aren't panning out.

Christy is disappointed, because people in Guam feel their plight has been neglected by the U.S. mainland. She wants them to know that someone has been thinking about them. But finally, she and her mom decide they'll just have to wait for the next disaster to hit the mainland. They don't have to wait long.

On February 23, a phalanx of tornadoes rakes across central Florida, killing dozens and destroying much of Kissimmee, near Orlando. Suddenly, Cheer Lift has its new destination. Carol gets on the phone again, and a company in Wilson, R&L Trucking, hauls the toys to Orlando.

And, for the first time, Christy is able to help distribute the toys and see the children's reactions first hand. Christy and Chad Pulley sign up as Red Cross volunteers. During spring break, a few days after Christy's 19th birthday, they drive to Orlando.

When they arrive at the distribution point, Christy jumps out of the car before it comes to a complete stop. Disney World has sent over some of its costumed characters. Pro baseball players take a break from spring training to sign autographs. Here's what Christy would later write about it:

"Everywhere you looked there were children cradling baby dolls and hugging teddy bears. Parents were reading the tags we attached to all our stuffed toys and dolls that say 'I have been well-loved by another child who now would like to give me to you. I hope you will love me too.'"

Thinking back on those memories, Christy still finds it hard to put her feelings into words.

"I was so overwhelmed to be able to get in the back of the truck and hand out the toys, to see those kids go away grinning from ear to ear," she says. "It was so wonderful."

Several weeks later, the warehouse shelves have filled back up with toys, not counting the dozens of boxes that have come in from the people in Pennsylvania and Ohio. All that Christy needs now is another group of volunteers to pack. The need, she knows, won't be far off.

"We're ready for the next disaster," she says.  ⤳

# One Mother's Challenge

## Betty Dishman

≈⊃⊂

As her cat Itchy quietly naps on her lap, Erica Hayes eagerly chats about learning the alphabet and sharing good times with friends at her preschool. Her blue eyes shining brightly, Erica gently strokes Itchy and says she even likes the "green stuff" (vegetables) she eats at school.

But there was a time when Erica, a Jackson County resident who just turned 5, wasn't having such a positive preschool experience. Her mother, Kimberly Hayes, remembers all too well when Erica used to cry every morning on her way to a local family day care home. And not only did Erica cry, she had problems sleeping and she wasn't developing even simple skills, such as cutting a piece of paper.

It was only when she moved to another day care and pre-

*Betty Dishman is a freelance writer living in Sylva, North Carolina with her two-year-old son, Aaron. She worked for six years as a newspaper journalist and served as an AmeriCorps VISTA Volunteer at three nonprofit agencies, including the AWAKE Child Advocacy Center in Sylva. She currently works in the Student Development Office at Western Carolina University and at the* Waynesville Enterprise-Mountaineer.

school which offered learning programs and practiced positive discipline techniques that Erica blossomed into a highly skilled youngster who looks forward to going to school.

Erica's story began a little more than two years ago, when her mother enrolled her in family day care. The day care provider in Jackson County treated the parents nicely, Kimberly says. At first, Kimberly observed no problems in Erica. But Erica was too young to articulate the difficulties she was experiencing.

"At two, it was still hard for her to express her feelings," Kimberly says.

A year or so later, however, Erica's mother and other relatives began to notice that Erica was developing problems with her behavior and sleep.

Kimberly began looking for reasons to explain Erica's behavior. She was surprised to find that the day care did not provide structured educational programs and that the children were allowed to nap at whatever time they wanted, rather than sticking to a scheduled nap time.

"She'd still be sleeping when I'd pick her up from my secretarial job at 5, and then she wouldn't sleep that night," Kimberly said.

Erica says she spent a good portion of the day watching television, rather than painting and drawing, as she does now.

The day care provider also resorted to corporal punishment. Though the day care was licensed by the state, and state regulations prohibit hitting children in a day care, Kimberly said the owner admitted to spanking the children when they had accidents during toilet training. Kimberly also learned the day care staff spanked the children for other trivial matters.

Although many parents did not object to this type of punishment and actually wanted their children spanked, Kimberly said it bothered her — especially spanking for toilet training accidents.

Kimberly discovered these things only after noticing their effect on her daughter. Kimberly first suspected that matters weren't right when she found Erica difficult to communicate with. And Erica's older sister noticed that Erica overreacted when she had toilet training accidents at home. It was at that point that Kimberly became concerned. She noticed that Erica had an extreme amount of energy. Although Erica tended to be energetic by nature, Kimberly worried that her daughter was more hyperactive than normal.

Finally, Kimberly's supervisor, Martha Smith — who was involved with Smart Start and other local children's programs — suggested Kimberly take her child to the Developmental Evaluation Center at Western Carolina University for testing.

"I didn't find out much," Kimberly remembers. "She passed all their tests and they said she had no developmental delays."

Concerned about her daughter's ability to sit still when she went to school, Kimberly consulted local school teachers. She asked the teachers if it made any difference whether or not a child had been in a family day care home or a day care center prior to attending school. Most of the teachers believed that it made no difference as long as the preschool environment had been stimulating, nurturing and safe.

Kimberly decided she was no longer willing to accept this child care situation as the norm, so she contacted a local child care resource and referral agency in an attempt to locate a better facility. Kimberly was put on a slow-moving waiting list. Her persistent calls hardly sped things along.

Finally, after many months of Martha's advocacy and Kimberly's persistence, Kimberly was able to tour some centers. Armed with the knowledge of the importance of a good day care, Kimberly was particular about the kind of care she wanted for Erica. Only one center appealed to her. She had to persist, however, until a space opened for Erica.

Once Erica began going to the new center, her life changed dramatically.

"She adapted almost immediately," Kimberly says, adding that Erica had almost no skills when she entered. Now Erica can write her name, cut paper, and draw. Toilet training went much more smoothly. Teachers have not noticed any behavioral problems with Erica, says her relieved mother.

"I feel more comfortable that the child can do what they ask her to do," Kimberly says. "They need to be able to sit down and participate in a group and Erica can do that."

Even though Erica is still somewhat hyperactive and doesn't always sleep through the night, Kimberly believes that these problems are not as extreme as they once were.

Asked what advice she would give other parents in her situation, Kimberly says parents need to go to the appropriate agencies in their communities and file complaints if they are not satisfied with their child care. (Kimberly later heard that the owner of the facility her daughter had originally attended had almost lost her license. The home is still operating.)

Although Kimberly believes some high quality family day care homes exist, she knows others are lacking. Having gone through appropriate channels to find the first day care, Kimberly says the state needs to do a better job of regulating the homes. She also advises parents to carefully screen the providers regarding their policies on discipline and other matters.

Kimberly is encouraged that the state has developed stricter educational requirements for day care workers, but says paying the workers better salaries would also help to improve the quality of child care. She would like to see hospitals and doctors give parents information on finding quality child care during pregnancy, and when children are born.

Finally, Kimberly says she was blessed to have an advocate such as her supervisor and believes all parents and children need one.

"The sad thing is mothers who don't have anyone to advocate for them," Kimberly says.

Meanwhile, Erica is happy and developing well. She says her favorite part of preschool is the "housekeeping center." And, she says, she wants to continue learning even more when she begins kindergarten next fall. &#x299B;

*The names in this story have been changed to protect the individuals' privacy.

# Unconventional School Unlocks Learning

## L  e  i  g  h      D  y  e  r

≈⌒

Andrew never really cared about school. He was smart enough to make B's and C's without even trying. But he could make $200 a day from selling drugs, and he preferred hanging out with his friends all night over cracking books.

When Andrew, 17, landed in the Mecklenburg County Jail last fall, he seemed destined to become a high school drop-out.

But instead of television and card playing, Andrew found himself studying Shakespeare and social studies.

He became one of the participants in a program that began in April 1997 — a Charlotte-Mecklenburg school campus inside jail.

*Leigh Dyer has been a staff reporter at* The Charlotte Observer *for two years, the last year as the public safety reporter. She has been a journalist for six years. She first became acquainted with Mecklenburg's jail school program in November 1997 and has made several visits to observe classes and interview participants. An article about the jail school originally appeared in* The Observer *on December 1, 1997.*

In this school, the uniforms are orange jail jumpsuits and flip-flops. There are no excused absences — attendance is mandatory. It doesn't matter if you were a dropout or expelled from school. If you're 16 or 17 and get sent to jail, you're going to go to class.

"It's hard work to come to jail now," said Jan Thompson, inmate program director for the Mecklenburg County Sheriff's Office.

Andrew is grateful for the second chance the program has given him. He made plans to rejoin the 11th grade after his release. He wants to be an architect and plans to apply to attend the University of North Carolina at Chapel Hill

He won't be satisfied with a GED equivalency degree. He wants his diploma.

"A diploma shows you worked hard for 12 years," he said in a low, determined voice, running his hand over his unruly braided hair.

He's made firm plans for after his release: "Try to get a job. Stay on the right path. Listen to my parents."

He said he knows where he went wrong. He wanted so badly to have friends and be cool that he didn't care about his future.

"People need to be focused," he said. "You be wanting to fit in with the crowd, but in the long run, you'll be better off with an education. You'll have plenty of friends later on."

The jail school has taught more than 300 students — some for just a day or two, some for several months. Some students have already been released, then come back again after being arrested on new charges.

The Charlotte-Mecklenburg school system budgeted about $60,000 to hire two teachers and purchase materials. The sheriff's office supplied the classroom space — a former commissary — and computers for the students.

The program is too new to show any firm results. But

Mecklenburg officials say it has already helped dozens of students who might have otherwise become dropouts keep up in classes.

Sheriff's department officials failed in their first attempt to win a grant from the Knight Foundation to hire case-workers to track the students after their release to see if the program made a difference in their lives. But they plan to keep applying for grants from other sources.

In the jail school, computer software leads the students through lessons in math, English, social studies, science or other subjects at their own pace. The computers don't have Internet access.

Students who are motivated to learn can get one-on-one time with the two teachers, C.W. Brown and Mona Saleh.

"I think for many of them we can provide them with some fleeting moment of support and idea of what the possibilities are," said Saleh.

When not working on computers, the students listen to lectures, fill out worksheets, do in-class reading and writing or watch instructional videos. After the "school day" ends, many inmates go on to other classes in substance abuse, teen health or life skills. Inmates are supposed to attend classes or group sessions from sun-up to sundown.

The program's leaders say it still needs work. Grades on jail lesson plans aren't yet transferable to other schools. But inmates can get their homework assignments from their regular teachers and get credit for them if they do them in jail.

The program was a shock for George, 17, who dropped out of school in the ninth grade. He hadn't been in a class for two years when he arrived at the jail to serve a 75-day sentence for an assault conviction.

"I haven't been to school in a while, so it was kind of an adjustment," he said.

But he doesn't mind the classes now. "It makes the time go by."

George grew up in Syracuse, N.Y., where he attended a strict Catholic school and was accustomed to being sent to the principal's office to copy pages out of the dictionary when he misbehaved.

But when he arrived in Charlotte at age 10, his lifestyle

changed. He fell in with a bad crowd, he said. At 15, he ran away from home and wouldn't come back until his mother promised she'd let him stay out of school.

"I always got good grades. I just didn't do the work, you know?" he said.

George keeps his eyes downcast as he talks. A tattoo of a marijuana leaf is partially visible on his chest under his jail uniform.

He tried to take a correspondence course but didn't finish it, he said. He got temporary work with a paint subcontractor.

He never expected to think about school again. But after 40 days in the school program, he's decided to try for his diploma when he gets out.

He plans to bring his folder of schoolwork home with him. He wants to show his mother he accomplished something in jail, he said.

If it weren't for the program, he said, "I wouldn't be thinking about going back to school."

Darryl, 18, made it part of the way through his senior year, but a series of arrests, beginning with one for cocaine possession in August 1997, made him think he'd wind up a dropout.

But he rediscovered school in jail and became determined to get his diploma. When he reached his 18th birthday, he wasn't required to attend the classes anymore. But he chose to stay in them.

"I spent 12 years in school. I don't want to waste that on a GED. I think that's sort of a lower level of education," he said, his eyes wide and hopeful. "I feel like shooting for a high school diploma, that will keep me out of trouble."

He's hoping to start his own business someday.

And he has advice for young people who might be tempted to take the path he's taken.

"School is the best way to go. It keeps you out of trouble." ≈

# Suitcases for Kids: Making a Difference One Suitcase at a Time

## Jennifer Kiziah

⤚⤙

S he's been on Oprah. Television stations and newspapers want to talk to her. She's frequently asked to speak to both large and small groups of people intensely interested in what she has to say. She receives mail and telephone calls from all over the country. And she's responsible for a project which has spread to almost every state in the nation — and several countries as well. She's accomplished all this and more, and she's only 13-years-old.

Aubyn Burnside, daughter of Dale and Linda Burnside of Hickory, gave new meaning to the phrase, "take the ball and run with it," when she began "Suitcases for Kids" in January 1997. In fact, shortly after its inception, Aubyn's efforts to provide every foster child in Catawba County with his or her

*Jennifer Kiziah, a reporter for the* Hickory Daily Record, *has covered Families for Kids and Court Improvement Project meetings during her two years at the paper. Attending the meetings has made her more aware of the importance of providing stable, loving families for foster and adoptive children and the challenges faced by those working to shorten the time-frame in which this may happen.*

own suitcase took on a life of its own, surpassing people's greatest expectations. Together, Aubyn and her "suitcase squad" have collected several thousand suitcases for children looking for homes. Aubyn and her "squad" continue to show adults and young people alike that someone doesn't have to be over 18, or even able to drive a car, to keep America's Promise to give something back to the community.

Aubyn's older sister, Leslie Burnside, joined the Catawba County Department of Social Services in December 1995 as the Families for Kids Performance Coordinator. She was hired after Catawba County was selected as one of eight sites across North Carolina to redesign the community's child welfare system. Funded by grants from the W.K. Kellogg Foundation, Families for Kids has five goals: providing accessible support for all families and children; creating a coordinated assessment for families and children; establishing one case manager or team for each child in care; providing one stable foster care placement for each child; and finding permanent homes for all children within one year.

While the intent of these goals is usually positive, the more immediate effects can be difficult for the children, especially when they are removed from their homes. The last two goals in particular require that the children move at least once. Often they drift through many placements before a more permanent home is found for them. When Leslie joined Families for Kids, she watched a national video from the Kellogg Foundation in which a social worker explains that it is common practice for social workers to put childrens' belongings in garbage bags when they remove the children from their homes. Leslie recognized that when social workers stuff a child's toys, clothes and other belongings into a garbage bag, it sends a message that his or her belongings have no value. On occasion, Leslie accompanied social workers when they removed children from their homes.

"In one case," Leslie remembers, "they used garbage bags, and in another they used plastic grocery bags." Either way, it sent a negative message to children already traumatized by having to leave familiar surroundings.

Even though DSS usually plans in advance to remove children from homes, rather than simply reacting to a crisis situation, the moves are almost always difficult on children, Leslie says. DSS may be involved with a family for a long time while it works to keep that family together. But, she says, efforts to keep families together do not always work out and a child may need to be removed. In those cases, DSS files a petition with the court. Then a social worker and law enforcement officer pick up the child from home or school and take him or her to a foster home. According to Leslie, if the removal takes place at the child's home, the social worker talks to the parent or parents about DSS's plan. "Sometimes the parents are cooperative and will tell the children to behave while they're away," Leslie says. "And sometimes the parents are very angry."

DSS tries to avoid placing children in foster care and sometimes tries to place them with relatives instead. It's difficult for the children to understand why they are being moved. Often it is because their safety is at risk. But sometimes, Leslie says, parents have their own problems and cannot adequately deal with the children's problems as well. Catawba County DSS's Family Preservation Unit has a good track record. In 1997, 501 of the 550 families the unit worked with stayed together. Thus, Leslie says, "when removal occurs, it basically means the family has not followed the service agreement" with DSS.

As one might imagine, removal is traumatic for the children because of all the unknowns involved. The children often ask questions which the social worker cannot answer. "Why does my mother drink so much if she loves me?" is one of those questions no adult can answer.

So, although it might seem a small comfort to the children,

Leslie asked her family for any old suitcases they could donate to DSS. That way, at least some of the children would
not enter an unfamiliar home with a garbage bag in tow. "I
didn't have the idea to start a whole program," Leslie says. "I
just had the idea to get a few suitcases from my family."

When someone asks Aubyn where she got the idea to collect suitcases for foster children, she basically says the idea
came to her because her sister, Leslie, kept asking their mother
to "get out the old suitcases and give them to her for the foster kids." Instead of disappearing whenever Leslie came to
visit, Aubyn decided to help by collecting some suitcases.
When Leslie told Aubyn she needed 300 suitcases for the
children in Catawba County, Aubyn started making plans.
Although she got the idea to begin a service project in November 1996, Aubyn decided to wait until after Christmas that year
to begin her project. She thought people might receive new
luggage as presents. If they did, she reasoned, they might be
more willing to recycle their old luggage for a good cause.

Describing her sister Aubyn as "a shy kid but very creative,"
even Leslie was amazed that Aubyn figured out how to network and get the project started. "She somehow came natu-
rally about how to do it grassroots," Leslie says. Although
homeschooled with her brother, Aubyn's extracurricular activities — especially in 4-H and Girl Scouts — had given her a
network of friends and contacts to put to work.

In the beginning, Aubyn, her mother, and younger brother
Welland, 10, were the only people working to fill the need.
Aubyn put notices in church bulletins, libraries, museums and
grocery stores about the need for suitcases. She asked fellow
4-H'ers and Girl and Boy Scouts for their help. To motivate
her friends, Aubyn asked them to imagine what they would
feel like if they were foster children, and were forced to move
what few belongings they had in black plastic bags.

After placing notices around town, Aubyn and her mother waited for about three weeks for something to happen. The Burnsides became somewhat apprehensive about the initial lack of response, so they purchased about 30–35 suitcases from the Salvation Army, Goodwill and yard sales. Then, Aubyn says, "All of a sudden churches started calling." Leslie says there was a deluge. "It really seems that within weeks she had enough for our department," Leslie says. "Kind of just out of the blue, there was this huge response. It didn't take long." According to Mrs. Burnside, they started receiving suitcases in early February 1997, and within two months they had 300 suitcases for Catawba County children. In addition to Aubyn, Welland and Mrs. Burnside's efforts, Aubyn credits some fellow 4-H'ers, Charlie and Isaac Meadows and Chris Young, with helping to collect the 300 suitcases for Catawba County DSS.

"Suitcases for Kids" made its first delivery of 171 suitcases in mid-March. At that point, they already had close to 300 suitcases but the suitcases kept coming — more than Catawba County needed — so the initiative moved into surrounding counties.

"The Meadows began collecting and storing suitcases at their house in Caldwell County about two months in," says Aubyn. At the same time, Chris Young began collecting suitcases to go to Cleveland County and Lincoln County.

Aubyn's little brother, Welland, guesses he became involved with "Suitcases for Kids" because he's part of the family, and he had to. But, he adds, he wanted to help. "I thought it'd be terrible to be in foster care, and even worse to carry my stuff around in a black garbage bag," he says. "I'd be embarrassed." In all, Welland estimates that he has helped collect about 3,000 suitcases since the project began. "It's hard work collecting and cleaning them," he says. "My sister and I have done most of the work, but everyone else has helped out a lot."

Chris Young, 16, lives with his mother, Leevada Young, in

Hickory. He became involved after Aubyn asked if he would mention it during some of the speeches he made. "I said, 'Sure,' and the next thing I know, I was in it," Chris says. He was named co-chairman of the Catawba County effort, while Welland was designated junior chairman. After agreeing to help Aubyn, Chris says, "I got on the computer and typed up bulletin inserts, mentioned it in speeches and talked to people in the community." As the only member of the original group who attends public school, Chris was unable to help with all the deliveries. As his time was somewhat limited, he had to make telephone calls about the project after he got home from school — usually after 5 p.m.

Chris said he probably made 15 to 20 speeches about "Suitcases for Kids" and was personally involved in making deliveries to at least five counties: Lincoln, Cleveland, Burke, Catawba and Caldwell. He believes all the hard work and effort was worth it, if only to show people that not all teens are self-absorbed. "The typical teenager now is supposed to get in trouble with the law and be up partying until midnight," Chris says. "They're surprised that there are good teenagers." Then he adds with a proud smile: "We are the future of America."

Charles Meadows III, 15, and Isaac Meadows, 13, live with their parents, C.W. and Melanie Meadows, in Granite Falls. After speaking to Aubyn, the brothers became chairmen of the Caldwell County suitcase drive. Charlie says they collected most of their suitcases from churches to which they sent fliers about "Suitcases for Kids." Isaac says they collected about 320 suitcases, and the family made deliveries to at least six counties: Alexander, Burke, Catawba, Caldwell, Watauga and Iredell. The brothers are also homeschooled, so they would load the van with suitcases and take off, homework in hand.

Mrs. Meadows approved of asking people for suitcases. "It's not like asking people for money," she says. "Most people are on a tight budget, but if you ask them for something they don't use, they'll give it." And, from the foster children's point-of-view, she says, giving suitcases to the children is a matter of contributing to their self-worth. Instead of putting their belongings in garbage bags, the children are given something of their own for their possessions, something that will not be taken back. "Suitcases for Kids" also gives families an opportunity to do something positive together, Meadows says.

And, while the Meadows say some children might hesitate before tackling what they think is a big project, they can still make a difference if they start small. "They couldn't solve the problem of foster children," says Mrs. Meadows, "but they can take care of them not having suitcases . . . one chunk at a time." She adds that when more people participate, individuals do not have to carry the whole burden.

Isaac believes the sooner parents involve their children in community service, the better. "If they start when they are five or six [years old], and say, 'This is easy,' they'll go on to something harder when they're seven or eight," he says. The Meadows believe it is important to help others because they may be the ones who need help tomorrow. "One day you're helping somebody, and the next they're helping you, and that's how society should be," Isaac says.

By April 1997, Aubyn had received so many requests for information on "Suitcases for Kids" that she developed a 12-page starter kit for people who wanted to begin their own project. Mrs. Burnside considers the project a guaranteed success. "It's not a question of whether people will respond," she says. "Just be prepared for an overwhelming response." And, while Aubyn attributes her success to all the people who helped her, she says the project is one that anybody can do. But, she cautions, "someone still has to be the leader and organize things."

With the suitcases, Aubyn has also gathered a number of stories about the crazy contributions and the great generosity of contributors. "We've gotten cardboard suitcases, purple, pink, round, make-up cases, duffel bags, and stuff," Aubyn says. She remembers a prayer circle in Lenoir that heard about the project, went to the Salvation Army, and bought 31 suitcases. Another time, she says, "My priest's godmother heard about it and mailed me some suitcases."

Charlie and Isaac say they've found everything from pennies to lingerie and knives in the suitcases. And Chris says

one company told him they had 35 briefcases they could donate, but they wanted to have them refinished so they looked
better. The shoe shop that refinished the briefcases even offered a discount when it learned what the company intended
to do with them, Chris says.

"Suitcases for Kids" became such a huge success, Aubyn
found other good uses for the thousands of suitcases she collected. In addition to donating plenty of suitcases to foster
children across the state, "Suitcases for Kids" donated suitcases
to ten children from Chernobyl — located in the former So-
viet Union — who visited Hickory in 1997. "They came over
with practically nothing, so we gave suitcases to them," Aubyn
said of the Belorussian children. Moreover, suitcases from the
project have traveled with medical teams to Guatemala and
Bolivia; with missionaries to Mexico; to Boys' and Girls'
ranches in Texas; to summer 4-H camps, and more.

Different organizations, businesses and groups have become involved with "Suitcases for Kids" as well. Mrs. Burnside
says post offices, city offices, sororities, department stores and
flight attendants are just a few of the groups that have offered
suitcases and help. Mrs. Burnside says she knows of at least
44 states that have picked up the idea. And one of Aubyn's
many pen pals has said she will try to begin a "Suitcases for
Kids" effort in Canada. Plenty of people are willing to help,
but the Burnsides have not yet found any person or organization willing to completely take over "Suitcases for Kids." According to Aubyn, "The only, and major, problem is that it
works too well." Mrs. Burnside, on the other hand, says dis-
tributing and storing the suitcases can be a problem. The
Burnsides ought to know; until recently their living room was
filled — floor to ceiling — with suitcases.

Now that her idea has helped numerous children and spread
like wildfire, Aubyn says her main goals are to make sure people
automatically recycle their old suitcases by taking them to their

local DSS, and to bring the need for families for foster children to everyone's attention. "In the future, I hope I won't have to do much," Aubyn said. "I hope they'll just automatically know what to do."

Aubyn and the others have slowed down their collection efforts a bit because Catawba and surrounding counties reached their saturation point. Chris doesn't see the project slowing down much, however. He's still inundated with suitcases.

"On my tombstone, it'll probably say, 'The Suitcase Man,'" he jokes.

Leslie still sends out about five or six starter kits every week. "Everybody wants information on it and a lot of parents have seen it's a good project for their children," she says.

Although Aubyn seems quite young to have accomplished so much, all she really did was identify a need and devise a way to respond to it. She has, however, shown by example that careful planning, publicity and a network of support can help anyone, young or old, achieve his or her goals. The Meadows offer some good advice for young people interested in making a difference but unsure about how to begin. Isaac urges action: "Go outside your home, look around and see what needs to be done, and get started," he says. Charlie, on the other hand, recommends finding a support system. "Try to get involved with community projects," he adds. All the young people say parental support and involvement contributed greatly to the success of "Suitcases for Kids." After all, somebody has to be the chauffeur. ⮑

# Larry's
# Kids

### C a s h    M i c h a e l s

⇒)⸦

**D**espite the crime, crumbling buildings, and the bad news always giving way to worse, those most impressionable and vulnerable — the children of public housing — have rarely been heard. More than anyone, they've absorbed the public housing experience. They've seen, heard, watched, and felt a lot.

They believe that not many people care how they're forced to live, and the few who may, can't really do much about it. They have dreams of not only being somebody in the future, but living out their childhoods today.

They dream, because they know the odds are against them.

And yet, as some of the children who live in Raleigh's Walnut Terrace public housing community in the shadow of downtown

---

*Cash Michaels is the managing editor and chief reporter/photographer for* The Carolinian, *the leading black newspaper in Raleigh, Durham and Chapel Hill. Last year, he was honored with the 1997 Excellence in Journalism Award by the N.C. Black Publishers Association. This story was adapted in part, with permission from "The Children of Walnut Terrace," a May 1997 article written by Michaels for* The Carolinian.

tell it, this is their home, and they are not afraid of it. "Home" to them is more than leaky pipes, big rats and broken playground equipment. The caring people and good friends in their community, they say, make Walnut Terrace home.

"I see these faces everyday," a 14-year-old resident told *The Carolinian*, a Raleigh black newspaper, in May 1997. "I consider everyone over here like family."

It is an impenetrable bond against the challenges of survival, and the intrusions of an outside world that's perceived as cold and uncaring. Being with one another, the children say, salves the indignity of being ignored. But sometimes, even that isn't enough.

Larry Cousar, 29, doesn't live there, but that doesn't mean he isn't welcomed. For over two years, the tall, slender young black man with the quiet demeanor and a clearly genuine love for kids has devoted at least three evenings a week, and sometimes even weekends (he is a case manager with Wake County Human Services full time), to providing after-school activities and guidance for the children of Walnut Terrace — a community many are quick to call "the projects," but which Larry will tell you is much, much more.

"There's sort of a misconception that these communities are like cesspools of violence, drugs . . . an area where there's no life," the native Philadelphian and St. Augustine's College alumnus says.

"But most of these kids, 99 percent of them, are really great kids, and there are some great parents in these neighborhoods. They, too, have their problems, a reflection of the greater society. For the most part, it's not really all that difficult to come into this community and be involved in the program, and give back to these kids."

That's why Cousar volunteers so much of his personal time toward the effort. By helping them gain a knowledge of self, he says, and showing them a black male role model who is

willing to share himself, Larry hopes to give to young African American children whom the rest of society has already written off, a chance not only to survive, but *live*.

"Community Connections," Cousar's program, is a pilot project of the nonprofit Reentry Juvenile Restitution. Originally designed to supervise the community service work of Walnut Terrace children who had been in trouble with the law and were on probation, Cousar eventually saw the need to make it more of a crime, drug, and teenage pregnancy prevention program.

"It's for the pure love of kids," he says. Recalling how he grew up in the tough public housing developments of Philly, he adds: "I just want to give them the gift of my experience, and hope that they wouldn't make the same mistakes that I made."

Children of low income communities many times fall prey to the evils of the streets because they don't see what other choices they have, Cousar says.

"[I try to teach them] better coping mechanisms [and] change their way of thinking, hoping that they'll grow a consciousness, educationally and emotionally.

"I just want to make sure they're growing positively."

Though the program is open to all the hundreds of children in Walnut Terrace, obviously all don't participate. On some days Cousar has as many as 25 or 30 playing both inside and outside the Lee Street Community Room where he's headquartered; at other times maybe only eight children will show up.

The important thing, however, Cousar says, is that all the children know that he's there for them, no matter what their ages, and that they're always welcomed. Despite having a wife and three young children of his own, Larry says the nine to 12 hours he spends a week in the program is meaningful, and makes a difference.

And he isn't the only one who thinks so.

Arnold Person, 12, is an East Cary Middle School sixth grader who dreams of playing basketball for the UNC Tar Heels one day while majoring in science.

"I like it because of experiments," he explains of his interest in science. "And you get to dissect cats and pigs," he says, to the probable chagrin of many animal lovers.

Arnold's best friend, James Chance, 13, is a seventh grader who also attends East Cary Middle School. He loves photography, plays football, and also hopes to attend UNC Chapel Hill. One day, he wants to be a police officer, "to get bad people off the street," he says. When he does, Chance won't be the first child from Raleigh's public housing to proudly wear a badge. Just ask the city's first black police chief, Mitch Brown, who grew up in nearby Chavis Heights.

Before they joined Cousar's Connections program two years ago, there wasn't much for children of Walnut Terrace to do, James and Arnold say, except stay in the house watching television or playing. True, the community center would be open, but no one really came to help them with their studies, take them on trips and to the movies, or teach them the discipline of community service.

"Larry's always here," Arnold says, indicating that the adult mentor is someone he can trust, depend on, and talk to. That makes Larry an important and positive influence in his life, the young man agrees.

James says he looks forward to going to the library Tuesday, Wednesday or Thursday afternoons, where they do homework or take part in programs. Larry stresses the importance of their studies, James says, a discipline he appreciates because it has helped him improve his grades.

"He makes me go get my homework," James says, reminded that Larry once told him he could get left back in school if he didn't do it.

"Larry and my parents . . . expect me to succeed. They care a lot about me."

"We learned about black history, and that people wanted to come out and [spend] time talking with us," Arnold said, referring to some of the community figures Larry has invited to speak to the children, like Raleigh's only black city councilman, Brad Thompson.

"Specifically I try to instill some sort of identity in them," Cousar says, regarding why black history is such a key tool at his disposal.

"In turn, I hope that will affect their behaviors . . . so when the [other] boys say, 'Yo, come on, let's go stick this store up,' I hope just a little part or a little piece of what I've shown them will tell them, 'Nah, I'm not going into that.'"

As any reporter who's covered a crime beat and interviewed prison inmates will tell you, most prisoners lament not having someone like Larry early in their lives to stay on them to do better. Many of them made their bad choices, they say, because they believed no one cared, and no one was there to listen.

Larry not only goes to the children of Walnut Terrace, but he's had many of them eat at his home, and they've had him over to theirs.

The boys' mothers, Mary Chance and Dorothy Turner, say they've definitely seen a difference since their sons got involved in Larry's program.

"He lets them see there's a different side of life," Ms. Turner, Arnold's mother, said, referring to field trips to the museum and other places. She now has hopes that her son will grow up to be an attorney.

"Exposure is a major part of learning," Cousar says. "A few weeks ago, we fed the homeless in Squirrel Park in downtown Raleigh in collaboration with the Eastern Stars [women's church group] and the undergraduate chapter of Groove Phi Groove at St. Augustine's College.

"It was a good experience because my kids got to see some young college students intermingle with grandmother-like images . . . and they got to see the plights of people that were a lot worse than theirs.

"It gave them a greater appreciation for what they have."

But just as in life, there is always time for games too, like "*Guester*," where the kids pick different color cards, and make each other guess what they're acting out. Both James and Arnold say neither is any good at it, but they keep playing anyway.

"And then on Saturdays, we get up at 10 o'clock and do community service, like pick up trash around here, and then go and eat," James says. "Sometimes on Sunday when the football season gets here, we watch the football game at Larry's."

"Sometimes, he takes us to the basketball games when he gets tickets," Arnold adds.

This mixture of studies, community service and fun gives

Larry's children a sense of belonging to something worthwhile, and in turn makes them feel worthy, lifts their self-esteem and willingness to achieve.

No longer do they have to act "bad" just because people who see them living in public housing expect them to. Now someone in their lives beyond their parents expects their best, Arnold and James say, and they like the respect they get when they give it.

It's the leverage Larry uses to talk to them about life and responsibility. Indeed, they've come to depend on Larry to show them a world they wouldn't see otherwise, and they seem to understand and appreciate his commitment to them.

It's not something they expect for an outsider to do, they say, but Connections kids have bonded with Larry because they know why he's there for them.

"To keep us off the street," James says.

"We've got somebody in the 'hood to help us," Arnold declares proudly. Both wish more adults from the African American community, many of whom have never taken the time to get to know the people who actually live in public housing, would volunteer just a few hours a week like Larry to teach them more about themselves, and the promise they have.

Nothing frustrates Cousar more about what he's doing, he says. He's almost given up asking black professionals, some of whom grew up in that very neighborhood, to come back to share an afternoon with the children. Many promise to stop by, then never show up.

"It's disheartening because it doesn't take a whole lot, but a lot of professionals think [they're] going to be burdened down or this is going to be a financial burden. [They think] if they spend time with 'this kid,' next week they're going to have to be paying his mother's light bill," Cousar laments.

It's symptomatic of a larger problem Cousar sees plaguing

his people, a problem that may cost African Americans a generation, if not more.

"The black community is so caught up in a materialistic, egocentric sort of mentality . . . that they've forgotten pretty much [everything] else," Cousar charges. "We're so out of touch with self, nothing else really matters, and our children are paying for it."

Cousar isn't the only one critical of his people. During a March 28, 1998 visit to Raleigh for a women's conference, actress Phylicia Rashad, best known for her portrayal of working mother "Claire Huxtable" on *The Cosby Show*, made it clear that she, too, believed that the black community has dropped the ball when it comes to doing more for its children.

"Where are we really going, if we have not invested power in our young people to believe in their own inherent goodness, [or] given our young people the true knowledge that God is living inside the human heart?" Rashad asked nearly 10,000 people gathered at the Civic Center. "Where are we going?"

"Our young people are not the problem; the problem is what our young people have not been given and we are the givers."

That absence of self is slackening the determination of young people, according to Cousar. "If more is expected of young people," Cousar says, "then the African American community is going to have to give more of itself to them.

"True, that your first obligation is to home, and to your family. But all I want is someone to come by and tell the kids what you do, and how you came about doing what you do. What was your plan, some of your experiences? It would probably take them 30 minutes, 40 minutes tops."

Larry's program isn't the only good one in Walnut Terrace or the Raleigh Housing Authority that works with young children at risk. And he has run into problems and barriers from time to time. But as he's quick to point out, many of the other programs have come and gone.

"A lot of programs come and they start up, the kids are really gassed up and hyped. But as the going gets rough, they fizzle," he says, thus leaving the children frustrated and accepting of dejection.

Some other programs have religious or other agendas that aren't necessarily about helping the children, he says. And few involve people from the larger African American community, its churches, or organizations.

Seeing more of their own people make time to make a difference would give these children a better, truer sense of what a real, caring "village" should be about, Cousar says.

Children like Arnold and James now have a better chance in life, thanks to Larry Cousar, and his dedication to their future. Though they're young now, a seed seems to have been planted — both say when they get older, they'll also volunteer their time, and give back to their community, so that other children will one day have the same chance they got.

"I will never forget what [Larry's] done for us," says James. ⌒

# CIS —
# A Personal
# Connection

## E l l e n   D i n g m a n

~⚭~

In middle school, Amanda felt she stood out in class —
but in an odd way. Even teachers noticed and treated
her coldly, she believed. She felt awkward, lonely, and
an angry frustration was building in her. Her self-doubt coiled
into rejection. She closed into herself and shrank away from
her classmates. She did not know what to do when she over-
heard them laughing at her or talking about her. She wanted
to slip away and disappear. Yet when excluded from their
activities, she cried.

But in high school a year later, her life changed.
Amanda quickly blossomed into a happy, caring, more confident teenager. Thanks to Communities in Schools, a program to which she was referred by her middle school teachers, she emerged as a warm, generous, open person, even

*Ellen Dingman is coordinator of the Communities in School program at
Garner Senior High School in Wake County. An educator for 25 years, she
has taught in Garner for 20 years and has coordinated the CIS program
since its inception eight years ago.*

as she coped with a turbulent home life.

"When I joined CIS in the 9th grade, I found people I could talk to. People who would listen to my problems and help me work them out, at home and with my classmates at school," she says. "I had someone to trust in the CIS staff. People to depend on."

When Amanda first came to CIS, we learned about challenges she faced everyday in her personal life, before she ever got to school. At times she didn't know what she would find at home. Those problems reached beyond her social life and into her school work. It was difficult for her to stay focused on learning.

"Sometimes I had to use all my energy to keep peace in the family," Amanda explains. "But there were times when I couldn't fix the confusion in my house. I was the one who tried to pull my family together. The pressures that I felt at home and at school were overwhelming. Going to school and facing other kids made things worse. I really needed the CIS staff at those times. Sometimes I cried; but I was able to vent with caring people and I could then go to class with less pressure. I learned to face my family's problems, deal with them, and grow beyond them."

Even when school seemed to be going well for Amanda, her home life often brought her down. Her 20-year-old brother, to whom she is closest, did drugs. Often he stole from home to support his habit. The VCR. The TV. Then worse. Burglary. He was found guilty of robbing a home in Washington, D.C. and sent to prison. Now he is clean and back home with Amanda and her mother. While Amanda believes he will succeed in the new life he is building, she anxiously feels his ups and downs.

Amanda's older sister is hardly in better shape. At 27, she took her five children and left her alcoholic husband, living for weeks in her car until it wrecked in an accident, and the young family found itself homeless. Amanda found them living near a dumpster behind the local Food Lion. Her sister had to buy water to wash the children. Amanda's mother finally agreed to take her oldest daughter and grandchildren into her home. But that was not a happy solution, and soon her sister and the children moved out and into a room with week-to-week rent. The instability of her sister's situation, and her temporary reunions with her husband, still worry Amanda.

Amanda is closest to her mother. She looks up to her with love and respect. But just as Amanda's life was pulling together, Amanda witnessed a freak drive-by shooting that seriously wounded her mother at a friend's outdoor birthday party. A stray bullet shattered her mother's leg, running inches from a vital artery, doctors say, before lodging in her back.

Through it all, Amanda has been able to find stability and a positive outlook, in large part through the CIS program that includes a volunteer tutor/mentor with whom she can celebrate her school successes such as becoming a school cheerleader.

In fact, Amanda has not only responded well, she excels in helping other students. Amanda has become a member of our county-wide CIS Youth Leadership Council. She volunteered to become a tutor/mentor in one of the local elementary schools and learned that she loved working with children. She developed into a bubbly, upbeat young woman who energetically helps younger students.

Despite her personal hardships, she maintains average grades. After graduation, she hopes to attend a community college, then transfer to a four-year college, so she can become qualified to teach school.

She continues to work part time after school as a grocery store cashier to help with her personal expenses. Her mother has recovered from her injury and, as a single parent, continues to work two jobs as a seamstress at men's clothing stores to support her family.

Programs don't change people; relationships do. CIS is all about relationships — from the very strong tutor/mentor component to the parenting sessions it offers families, the weekly breakfast club that fills social as well as nutritional needs, the quarterly ice cream celebrations of grades and attendance, and the one-on-one positive relationships offered by the CIS team to young people like Amanda.

Amanda is successful because of who Amanda is, and because CIS helped her believe in herself. She has become a stable young woman with a hopeful future. She is ready to move beyond her family's challenges to her own personal rewards and experiences. We wish her well and look forward with confidence to her future. ⌒

*Amanda is an alias.

# The Mask Removed: De-Jing Dong Finds Himself Again in America

## Barbara Thiede

≈⌢

D e-Jing Dong became a different person this year, because he finally found the freedom to be the person he once was. De-Jing has begun talking and joking again, like any 11-year-old. Again, his laughter ripples like a slender waterfall.

De-Jing neither talked nor laughed when he came to Concord, N.C., three years ago — not in public, anyway. His first two years in American elementary schools were marked by an almost complete silence.

"In fourth grade — if he was mad or happy — I would have no idea," says his best friend, Tyler Treadaway. "He always had the same expression. He would just block it."

*Barbara Thiede spent too many years pursuing her Ph.D. in comparative German and American history. Now she works too many jobs. Among them are public relations writer and freelance journalist, personal columnist for* The Charlotte Observer's *regional bi-weekly, "Cabarrus Neighbors," and coordinator for the 1999 Reed Gold Mine Bicentennial. She has been married for 16 years and has one son.*

De-Jing's fourth grade teacher, Lori Westerholt, found him just as enigmatic.

"I didn't know if he understood me," says Westerholt. "I didn't know what to do. I felt bad for him. I felt guilty."

De-Jing refused to answer Westerholt's questions. He hardly ever made eye contact with her, either. De-Jing hung his head. He always walked behind his teacher. He maintained the same inexpressive demeanor almost all the time, his face as still as a mask.

Not now. This year, De-Jing's fifth grade teacher, his best friend and his own growing ability to communicate are bringing him back.

Teachers have always found De-Jing polite, well-mannered and quiet compared to their louder students. De-Jing, on the other hand, claims he was an outgoing and talkative child, "until I got to America. [Then] I was shy. Scared, 'cause I don't know how to speak any English."

De-Jing moved to the U.S. from Fuzhou, a city in eastern China just across the Strait of Taiwan. He was sent for by his parents, who had accepted a work offer from a Chinese restaurant and settled in Concord three years earlier.

Following a Chinese tradition still quite common even in full "westernized" areas like Taiwan, the Dongs had left their two children — five-year-old De-Jing and his three-year-old sister Wang-Juan — with their paternal grandparents until they could establish a household of their own. De-Jing's younger sister is not yet with him, and the children's ongoing separation continues to cause De-Jing particular pain.

Chinese immigrants were long prevented both by law and by social practice from forming families in America. Chinese laborers who came to America before 1883 could neither bring their wives nor marry Caucasians. As a result, the Chinese population remained predominantly male and transient for decades. Many immigrants spent 20 or 30 years earning as much money as possible and then returned to China to buy land. It took generations for the Chinese to develop thriving "Chinatowns" with equal numbers of men and women in large cities such as Los Angeles and Chicago.

De-Jing's parents, however, did not settle in a big city, where they could have relied on other Chinese immigrants to soften the confusion of culture shock. Instead, they came to Concord, a small town that had a population of 30,809 in 1992. A few years after they had arrived, they started their own restaurant and take-out, the Dragon Palace.

Concord was a quintessentially Southern small town until Charlotte burst its seams in neighboring Mecklenburg County in the late eighties and early nineties. In Concord, the first question still asked of anyone who looks or sounds different establishes clear-cut cultural borders: "You're not from around here, are you?"

De-Jing arrived in a world that knows little about culture shock or the painful process of immigration. Folks "from around here" have lived in Cabarrus County for three generations or more. Most people are white and Protestant. Catholic newcomers insist that many older Concordians have just begun to accept them as fellow Christians. And old timers rarely meet anyone they think might "speak Jewish."

De-Jing found Concord too much to cope with at first. The language was not merely unfamiliar — it was radically different. The culture was not just new, it taught the opposite of what he had known. No wonder De-Jing lived in a state of cultural shell shock for nearly two years.

At first, his silence was deafening.

"I would have felt worried about any student that was as quiet as he was," explains De-Jing's fifth grade teacher, Kristi Teal. "He wouldn't respond to questions at all. If you put it different ways, most kids will respond back. De-Jing would just not say anything. It wasn't, 'I don't understand.' It was complete silence."

De-Jing had no way to guess at the meaning of a word or even at the way it ought to be pronounced. In De-Jing's native Min or in his second language, Mandarin Chinese, a typical syllable is formed with one consonant and one vowel. An English syllable can appear positively bizarre from a Chinese vantage point — something that probably sounds to the Chinese ear like a mass of stones and pebbles knocked together. The word "strengths," for example, includes three consonants, one vowel, and three more consonant sounds.

The very structure of De-Jing's native language precluded guesswork. De-Jing's Chinese dialect has little in common with English other than subject-verb-object word order. His language experience was almost useless in America. In effect, De-Jing entered a linguistic vacuum. De-Jing's English as a Second Language teacher, Annette Widelski, could not have been expected to have any experience or training in Chinese, much less De-Jing's native Min.

But it wasn't just language that separated De-Jing from this new world. De-Jing had come from a world with hardly any cars, to one that was ruled by them. He had gone from a world where no one "had much money," to a world where his parents could buy a house and a car and still send money home to China. In De-Jing's homeland, he says, each U.S. dollar would have eight times the purchasing power it does in America.

His world had been a big city made of dull gray or brown high-rises, the kind that tower over narrow streets filled with bicycles and pushcarts. Hardly any trees, bushes, or flowers graced the streets — there was no room for them.

De-Jing lived in the mountains of Eastern China, in a country where deference is good behavior, where looking straight into someone's eyes signals a challenge. In China, walking next to your teacher suggests presumption.

But human emotions are the same in any culture. After two years of apparent impassivity, De-Jing found ways to show his.

He had two friends who helped him. His fifth grade teacher looked for ways she could ease his isolation. Kristi Teal took De-Jing on short trips outside class, and shared her personal and family life with him. A fellow student, Tyler Treadaway, felt De-Jing's distress and alleviated it by becoming his friend.

Teal had had some experience teaching students who were not "from around here." But most of her truly foreign students were Spanish-speaking, and there were enough of them at the school to form a peer group for support and comfort.

De-Jing was different.

"There wasn't really anybody else," she points out.

During the 1994–95 school year, there was only one Chinese student attending a public school in Cabarrus County. In 1995–96, De-Jing arrived, one of three Chinese students. The following year, the number remained steady. This past year, the school system started out with two Chinese students. But by spring, one family had left, and De-Jing was truly alone.

Soon after the school year started, Teal went to see the principal at the school, Scott Padgett. They talked about De-Jing's silence, and his isolation.

Teal and Padgett went to visit De-Jing's parents at the Dragon Palace, and they brought De-Jing along to translate. Teal got permission to take De-Jing out on an excursion now and then — to dinner, to an indoor jungle gym, or to a school event. She was even allowed to take De-Jing home to meet her own two-year-old.

"She takes the cares and the concerns of the schoolroom home with her," Padgett says. "In this sense, she literally took him home."

The second time Teal arranged an outing, she wondered if a different De-Jing had climbed into her car.

"It only takes about 10 minutes to get to my house from school," she explains. "And he is non-stop talking the whole way. He talked about everything under the sun."

De-Jing calls his teacher his friend.

"She's nice," he says. "She's not mean." When he knows he's going on another outing with his teacher, De-Jing is happy, excited.

Almost immediately De-Jing translated his gratitude into the kind of work that could make him a successful student.

"He started turning in assignments," Teal said. "At the beginning of the year I didn't get anything. Now, it's no problem. Now I get permission slips and homework."

De-Jing is motivated. He asks his parents to sign permission slips so that he can come back to school for evening programs, or go on a field trip. He capitalizes on his strong subject, math, but he turns in his work for social studies and reading, too.

The voluble, extroverted boy De-Jing says he had been in China finally arrived in America. He brought all of his emotions with him.

Neither his fourth grade teacher nor his best friend, Tyler, can remember seeing De-Jing downright unhappy in fourth grade. But in fifth grade, struggling to participate, to understand, De-Jing was able to express frustration and pain instead of hiding behind an expression that revealed nothing.

One day, Kristi Teal returned to the classroom after a special teacher had visited the class. De-Jing was crying.

Apparently, the visiting teacher had tried to get De-Jing to respond, and when he didn't, the teacher responded with a phrase De-Jing knew well: "Don't you understand what I'm saying?" the teacher asked.

"It wasn't said forcefully," says Teal, "but it just shut him down."

Crying, laughing, or talking in a new language — those acts

of emotional openness were De-Jing's first voluntary steps into his strange new world. He took many of those steps in an after-school program, Kids Plus.

De-Jing knew a couple of the kids in the program. They had been in his fourth grade class, too. One of the children was Tyler, whose father Sam, is an assistant principal at Northwest Middle School in Cabarrus County. His mother, Resa, works as an account manager with the hazardous waste company Ecoflo. Tyler had been De-Jing's partner on a couple of class projects in fourth grade, and he knew then that De-Jing was having problems.

"He was real quiet," Tyler says, "and just wouldn't answer. At first he wouldn't do anything. He wouldn't try very often to do the worksheets the teacher gave us. He was pretty shy and wouldn't talk to me much."

That changed the following year when Tyler started helping De-Jing with his homework in Kids Plus. When Teal found out that De-Jing had a friend in the program, she tried to help deepen the relationship. She asked Tyler if he would consent to a formal working relationship, as De-Jing's official tutor.

"Tyler felt special when he was asked to tutor De-Jing," says Resa.

"It helped him learn some of the lessons the teacher has assigned him, because teaching is the best way to learn."

Tyler took the time to teach, but also the time to listen. It was easy: He liked De-Jing.

"He's real nice and he's never really put down anybody," Tyler says. "He's always trying real hard when he does his homework to get good grades. He does his homework a lot now."

Tyler noticed that De-Jing hasn't had an easy transition to America.

"I ask him things about China. I think he sort of misses it. I asked him, say something in Chinese. He never talks about it. He doesn't like that subject a lot."

But other topics are open game for jokes or commentary.

"He shares his feelings with me a lot," Tyler says. "He's like, 'I don't like the cafeteria food.'"

Now, De-Jing will even talk to strangers — even about his homeland. If you ask him what he misses, though, he won't mention friends or favorite places. His mind closes in on one thing. "Playing there with my sister," he says. Then he adds, quietly, "when I'm 13, she might come here."

The answer to "what do you miss about China" is always the same, no matter who asks it: Wang-Juan.

Still, De-Jing can think past that pain. Recently, he got involved in a 4-H talent show. Tyler and a couple of friends sang to "Cuban Pete," a tune from Jim Carrey's MASK. De-Jing played the group's manager. Tyler even gave De-Jing a name: "Rapmaster Dong." De-Jing will travel with the other kids to Gastonia, for the regional 4-H competition.

Tyler talks about De-Jing every day, Resa says. She, too, can tell that De-Jing has changed. Last year, when she drove past him walking home from Kids Plus, she would tap her horn and wave.

She got almost no response. "He hung his head," she says. Not this year, though. "Now," Resa says, "he waves back."

When Tyler got a chance to interview De-Jing, the two boys focused entirely on each other. De-Jing looked straight into Tyler's eyes. It was a conversation of equals, during which De-Jing admitted that the worst thing about America was pizza.

"Until I ate it." he said. "[It] smells bad, and then I ate it and it smells better," he said.

(Later, after Tyler ran out of questions, the two boys wondered if the worst thing about America was being asked a lot of questions.)

De-Jing says he wants to be a policeman when he grows up. Asked if he chose the profession because he'd always know what to wear, and could even wear the same clothes every

day, he took the opportunity to make a wry joke.

"Would wash them, though."

At the end of the school year's third quarter, De-Jing went to assembly, sat down with the other kids, and waited for the distribution of buttons and pencils for perfect attendance and the announcements of high scorers in the accelerated reading program. Two members of the Kiwanis Club were there, to pass out the quarter's "Terrific Kids" award, a diploma given to children who have demonstrated solid citizenship and exemplary behavior during the previous nine weeks.

De-Jing's name was called. He was a "Terrific Kid."

"He was just aglow that day," remembers Kristi Teal

"He was like, astonished," says Tyler Treadaway.

Next year, De-Jing will start at Concord Middle School. He'll be one student in a class of about 330 students instead of one of just 77. He'll be 13 when he graduates.

Maybe his little sister, Wang-Juan, will be there at the ceremony. ⬲

# Hope, Love, Charity...
# and Basketball

## Paul Bonner

⁓⁣⁓

The teenagers, all of them young men, sit around a table and, after the fashion of teenagers, try on different ethical stances as they might pairs of jeans at the mall. Syvil Burke is like the shopping companion who waits outside the dressing room and comments on the style and fit. She has a definite look in mind, that of the Good Samaritan in Jesus' parable, which she has recounted to start the discussion.

Can any of them tell her what unconditional love is?

"It's when you care deeply about someone," one teen says.

"Like you might take a bullet for somebody," suggests another.

This is not out of the realm of possibility for these teens. It happened about a year earlier in an incident some of them heard about. A young man dove in front of his mother to shield her during a drive-by shooting and was wounded.

*Paul Bonner is a reporter for* The Herald-Sun *and a freelance writer. He lives in Durham with his wife and two sons, Andrew (18) and George (11).*

The discussion takes place on a Sunday evening in a classroom at the YMCA in Durham, across town from where that shooting happened. These young men have come both from that neighborhood and from all over the city, brought in vans by volunteers.

They are the beneficiaries and constituents of Operation Hope, one of the more free-standing of Durham's several organizations and agencies that, in the language of social workers, provide services to children at risk. The risk, always left undefined, is nonetheless vivid enough to the teenagers whom the phrase describes, despite their age group's generally observed belief in its own invincibility. Robbery, assault, theft, murder, addiction, racial discrimination, hatred, parental apathy — they all are expressed as probabilities by the phrase, which implies that if the teens haven't yet experienced these things, they will eventually.

In response to Burke's question, the teens let loose enough theological red herrings to fill a net to bursting.

If someone punches you in the gut, do you have to love them? If so, does that mean the punch is divinely ordained?

"You need to be kind to everyone, because you don't know, that punch may never come," Burke tells them.

"The punch always comes," one teen mutters under his breath.

As Arthur West, Operation Hope's founder and director, puts it: "These are not little Sunday school kids we're dealing with."

To the youngsters he is Coach West. He is closely identified with Operation Hope, providing its impetus and commanding its primary activity, basketball.

Besides the discussion group, there is another group of teens meeting in a nearby kitchen. They're the ones who are here because a judge said they had to be, as a condition of probation or release pending trial. One of them is sitting slumped forward, head down, staring at the floor. Arthur says it's because he's chagrined at having to share the cramped space with a member of a rival gang. In another room are children as young as 10, including a few girls.

After classroom time, they all enter the gym and sit in the bleachers. West, speaking into a microphone hooked to a small portable amplifier, talks about the upcoming state basketball tournament they'll enter in Greensboro.

"If I see one person causing a disturbance, I want Bob to take you home or the van to take you home, because I know where you're headed next — downtown," he warns. Bob is Bob Appleby, a retiree and Durham County Republican Party chairman who also is the chairman of Operation Hope's board. Downtown means jail.

"The first thing you've got to have is a good — what?" West asks.

"Attitude," the teens respond in unison.

This will be proper basketball, not street ball, but a disciplined game, with drills, he says. He leads them onto the floor for practice in layups, dribbling and shooting.

"Move!" he shouts.

West is middle-aged and stocky, and speaks his mind freely. He suspects that social work professionals look down on him and Operation Hope because he lacks their academic training. Some of them, however, have said that his bluntness and freedom from bureaucratic constraints and ways of doing things make him more effective than those confined to official channels.

West knows how to communicate with these teenagers. He knows the pressures they face and he knows about getting off track. West grew up partly in Chicago, where he was a member of the Blackstone Rangers street gang. He later joined the Marines and did a tour of duty in Vietnam.

He started Operation Hope in fall 1996 after Sedric Alston,

a 19-year-old still known to some in Operation Hope, was shot and killed by another teen. The "Hope" in Operation Hope is an acronym for Helping Others Progress Effectively. At first, West rented a city-owned gym at a recreation center, until a Durham Parks and Recreation director and one of the officials who applauded his maverick approach, Carl Washington, arranged for the group to use the gym free and provided vans for transportation. When Washington died suddenly from a heart attack only weeks later, West says, he lost his most valuable ally.

He scrounged money for uniforms from a bar and grill beside the rec center. He walked the streets of the area, talking to young men and inviting them to play basketball. There were 16 of them at first, and they won every game they played against city rec teams and other leagues. He listened to them, trying to head off violence before it started whenever he received a hint that something was about to happen. Several Durham churches joined him, providing donations and helping with transportation. Most important, their members, like Syvil Burke, volunteered their time. West worked as a janitor at Duke University or construction contractor to support himself while spending most days visiting the courthouse, sitting in juvenile court, passing around his business card to parents there, or going to schools to speak to kids he'd heard could play ball and needed some guidance. More recently, Operation Hope began receiving a small but regular grant from a state-funded but locally administered pot of money called Community Based Alternatives. For the first time, West received a salary from Operation Hope and began working for it full time.

It was from one of those school visits that the Coopers learned about West and Operation Hope. Shirley Cooper heard that West had visited her older son, Carlos. She had heard of West before and called him. She asked him if her younger son,

William, could join Operation Hope, too. William plays basketball every chance he gets. He probably could make the
team at Riverside High School, but his home is a long way
from the school, and his mother wants him to limit his time
on the sport and keep up his grades. Next year, as a senior,
he'll probably try out for the school team, but when the season is over, Shirley Cooper wants her son back in Operation
Hope.

William says his first visit to Operation Hope in November 1997 was "all right," but he wasn't sure he wanted to stick
with the group at first. Seated in a living room of his family's
house with his mother and her fiancé, Gary Bracey, William
says he was afraid he would be sitting on the bench during
Operation Hope's games. He plays basketball nearly ever day
at one court or another within walking distance from his
home. His electives at school are both in physical education.

He soon found his fears about Operation Hope were unwarranted, and he got to play. Meanwhile, he grew to respect West, overlooking West's outspokenness, observing that West was equally prone to listen to his and other youths' ideas and concerns and to support them when they were right.

"Most coaches don't want to hear what you have to say," William says, adding that Coach West is different.

William, 16, hasn't been in any trouble with the law, and "we're just trying to keep it that way," Shirley Cooper says, as her mother, Arie Long, sets a skillet to sizzling in the adjoining kitchen. Busy traffic on Alston Avenue can be heard through the house's outside wall.

William says he knows other young men in Operation Hope who have been on criminal probation, and he's noticed a change for the better in them. One of them "has been calmed down," he says. "He would snap at you and cuss you out," he says. "He doesn't do it as often now."

Shirley Cooper says that Operation Hope underscores the message she tells her sons: that they are under rules, that they need book learning along with sports, that they should heed their elders' wisdom, that certain places and people are best avoided.

West has noticed William's good attitude, that he didn't argue with him on the court. "In Operation Hope, he is a reconciler and does what Coach says without arguing," says Appleby, the board chairman. This spring, West arranged for William to receive a plaque: Operation Hope's citizenship award for the year. In a ceremony at a local church, William received the plaque from Durham's mayor, along with a trophy for being the most valuable player of the city basketball league.

Elaine O'Neal is a District Court judge who sees Operation Hope as a way to extend her court's supervision of young people. She met West when they worked together on a school task force on students with behavior problems. She already had read about him in a local newspaper.

"He impressed me as a man with a passion for kids," O'Neal says.

She noticed him in the courthouse several times a week, checking on the cases of children and teens he was working with. He didn't have to be there, she realized, and interpreted this as a sign of personal commitment. She decided to start referring young defendants to his program.

"Most of the kids, they just want somebody to care about them," O'Neal says. "They don't care whether they have a Ph.D. or whatever."

Moreover, she said, action too often is disjointed among courts, schools and all the other agencies in which children's lives can be enmeshed. One agency often doesn't know what the other has done, and sometimes neither knows what the child is really up to. Delays are inevitable between the time a juvenile court counselor learns that a child has violated his probation and the time the worker can write up the violation and send it to the court. A juvenile court counselor in Durham carries an average load of 43 cases, among the highest in the state, she says.

Rehabilitation, when applied to juveniles, fails to take into account a fundamental problem, O'Neal says: "Some of these kids have never been *habilitated.*"

Furthermore, the court docket is often crowded. Three weeks might elapse before O'Neal learns a child has violated parole and five more weeks before the judge's rotation in juvenile court brings her back to the bench from district court to do something about it. In the meantime, the child begins to believe the court won't enforce its orders. But from West, she said, she can learn about a child's compliance — or lack of it — within a day or two.

"That type of turnaround is crucial," she said. "In juvenile court, you have to be innovative."

A need for innovation hardly begins to describe West's prescriptions for "the system."

"To me, the system is destroying these kids," he says. "They need to scare them. They're not scaring them."

A 17-year-old referred by O'Neal to West on pretrial release from jail illustrates another difficulty: many talented, smart youths can say all the right things and yet demonstrate in their actions the two-steps-forward, three-steps-back course that makes their caseworkers sigh and shake their heads. The 17-year-old keeps vacillating between duty and caprice. Before getting into Operation Hope, the youth had been habitually truant from school. At first he professed to enjoy Operation Hope and school, which he re-entered. In both places, he proved himself to be a model of respect and decorum. But a week later, he failed to show up as required for Operation Hope's Sunday evening sessions and after-school counseling. He quit going to school. A few days later, West learned that a burglary victim had noticed the youth wearing her stolen jewelry.

West has had worse disappointments. Two brothers who dropped out of Operation Hope were charged early in 1998 with participating in the robbery and murder of a taxi driver. West says he tried, before the crime, to get the brothers to return to the program, but without success.

Increasingly, he focuses on younger teens, like Seneca Caldwell, who is 14 and a starting guard on West's younger basketball team. Like William Cooper, Seneca has a clean record, but he knows teens who bring guns to school

"That's why I try to keep him busy," says Seneca's mother, Debra Caldwell.

Seneca enjoys basketball and drawing. He makes friends easily, but like many impulsive young people, can be easily discouraged. Watching television one day, he saw an advertisement for an art correspondence course and dialed the number on the screen. Several days later, a woman showed up at the family's home to sell them the course, says his mother. Debra Caldwell was glad to pay for anything that could channel her son's raw talent into a useful activity.

But now, looking at the drawing lessons, Seneca says he's not sure he'll continue. It looks too hard, he says.

West, sitting with the family in their living room, tells Seneca he should continue what he started.

Later, in the YMCA gym, Peter Wando, a volunteer with Operation Hope, says, "the key is to influence these kids before they get into trouble." Appleby says that's best done by being firm but fair with them.

"There's a thing called tough love," Appleby said. Like Wando, he feels that his time spent with the youngsters is the best investment he can make in this group's future. "I guess the reason is, there but for the grace of God go I. I could have so easily gone the way some of them do, in the environment I grew up in. I would like them to see people who are not part of their environment who are interested in seeing that they're going to get a fair shake." ☞

# For Himself,
# His Community
# and His Country

Iris    Carter    Gross

≈⁓

A t first glance, his achievements are overwhelming. Grant Erskine excels in academics and sports. He is active in church and Boy Scouts; works part-time; and recently completed 1,227 hours learning about himself, his community, America and the world to earn the Bronze Congressional Award. His resume is already more impressive than most adults who have lived three times his lifetime.

"If most of us could have accrued 1,227 volunteer hours in a lifetime, we would have accomplished something," U.S. Representative Richard Burr said during Erskine's award ceremony.

Despite all his achievements and awards, Erskine remains focused and humble.

"It didn't seem like that much work because I did it at my own pace and did what I wanted to do," says Erskine. "Time

*Iris Carter Gross is a North Carolina native, raised in Greensboro where she still lives with her two children, Elizabeth (12) and Brice (9). A graduate of Guilford College with a B.A. in English and a communications concentration, Iris is the news editor for* The Messenger, *a bi-weekly newspaper for western Rockingham County.*

goes fast as long as it's what you want to do."

Living in Madison, a small town in western Rockingham County 30 minutes north of Greensboro, Erskine has immersed himself in the community.

"A lot of people in rural areas don't get the chance to do things urban kids do," says Erskine. "I've had the chance to compete with the best of them and that's good."

Students from Dalton McMichael High School attended the celebration along with dignitaries such as Superintendent Dr. George Fleetwood, Principal Joe DeVault, Rockingham County Board of Education Chairman Jeff Eanes and the Erskine family.

"Not all recognize there are very few people in this country that commit the time to their community, their state and their country," says Congressman Burr. "This is the first award I've had the honor to present and glad I've had the opportunity to do it."

Erskine first heard about the Congressional Award program after earning his Eagle Scout rank at age 12 (the median age for Boy Scouts achieving Eagle rank is 15). At the time, he put the information about the Congressional Award aside, he says. In May 1996 he decided to begin working on the requirements.

Broken down into age groups and service hours, the bronze award is given to students over age 14 who provide a minimum of 210 hours of activity over seven or more months.

Hours are divided among four categories: volunteer service, personal development, physical fitness and expedition. Adults must supervise the program as a "validator."

Although his original goal was to complete 100 hours of voluntary service within a year, Erskine put in 422 hours from May 1996 to June 1997 with Boy Scout Troop 562, under the supervision of Assistant Scoutmaster Timmy Tilley.

"I think everybody should try to do something to serve," says Erskine. "Service is where I got a lot of my leadership skills. Kids are all different — you have to stick with it . . . they begin to trust you. It's good to know someone looks up to you in a positive way."

Erskine became a world traveler to gain hours in expedition/exploration. Eyeing a trip through Italy, Austria and Hungary at a price tag of more than $4,000, Erskine raised the money on his own.

Organizing a corporate fundraising volleyball tournament for the Air Force Junior ROTC, of which Erskine is a member, Erskine collected entry fees, sold concessions and collected admission to raise $1,000. Area clubs also provided donations for Erskine's trip. In exchange, he gave speeches about his experience.

"It was a good trip and it made me appreciate different cultures," Erskine says.

Visiting Hungary, a country previously in the communist block, shook up some of the students, said delegation leader and validator Fran Hamilton.

While most of the students were shocked by the poor conditions, "nothing we came across phased him (Erskine)," she said. "He sailed through it."

Aiming to improve his overall fitness level, Erskine worked to improve his time for running the mile. He also joined the cross country and indoor track teams at McMichael, played soccer, and lifted weights.

By linking his interest of aeronautics to personal development, Erskine sought to improve his knowledge of model rockets by joining the aeronautics club.

In addition to these activities, Erskine has a cumulative grade point average of 4.4 out of 4.0 and is fourth in a class of 218. He works part time for Madison-Mayodan Recreation Department, is an active member of the youth group at Mayodan

First Baptist Church and belongs to various other clubs at school. After high school, Erskine hopes to receive an appointment to the United States Air Force Academy in Colorado Springs, Colo., where he'd like to major in space operations.

"After the Air Force, I want to be in public service and be a politician," he says.

"Now you can see why I'd not like to see him run for Congress against me," jokes Congressman Burr.

While many young people feel external pressure to excel, Erskine says his motivation is self-generated.

"I've had a lot of people in my life, but not just one person," he says. Guidance from his parents has helped "keep me going," Erskine adds. "Most of what they did started when I was real young — instilling some good values in me.

"I have always known he was destined for great things," says his mother, Marsha Erskine. "I expect a lot from all my children, and if you expect a lot, you get it."

Grant's father, Marty Erskine, is a plant manager at Burlington Industries. He knows his son's volunteerism isn't simply for kudos. Grant "will continue to do these things even though the awards are over," says Marty. "Grant is very driven and very focused — many times we don't know what he is doing until he has done it."

The Erskines do not to push their younger sons, Clark who is 13, and Craig who is seven, to fit into their brother's mold, says Marsha.

"They are each special in their own way," she adds.

Participating in so many activities may seem tiresome, but Erskine says it is his form of relaxation.

"School gets me down sometimes," he said. "But this is my way to relax. I also like to go out and play sports, go camping, mountain biking — anything outdoors."

As junior assistant scoutmaster for Troop 562 in Mayodan, Erskine has earned the respect of both elders and peers.

"Anything you ask him to do, he'll do it," says Tilley.

In helping scouts, Grant will assert his ideas, even if they are different than the adult leaders. If the direction seems odd, the leaders follow the idea and everything always turns out okay, said Tilley.

"Everyone takes his word just like an adult's."

Many of the scouts have worked with Grant for several years, learning about merit badges and projects under his leadership.

"He (Grant) and my brother are the two people I look up to," says Boy Scout Bryan Hayes, who is in the seventh grade. "He's everything I ever wanted to be — he's da bomb."

As an eighth grader, Johnny Gilbert also respects and relates to Grant.

"A lot of scouts act like they are higher than you, but he's on your level," he says. When approaching the brink of trouble, Gilbert reflects on what Grant would do in the same situation. "Sometimes I catch myself thinking about what he's done."

Tenth grader Jared Kallam also looks to Grant as an example. "Grant tries to get along with everybody," says Kallam. He doesn't hesitate "to talk to somebody just because they aren't in the group. Everybody respects him."

Neal Bullins is also in 10th grade, grew up with Grant and attends scouts, school and church with him.

"He's a good friend; you can trust him," says Bullins.

Grant has a lighter side and enjoys a practical joke, he adds.

"He'll play jokes on you, you play jokes on him."

At the same time, Grant sets limits for himself and others.

"I've done a couple of crazy things," says Bullins. "If it's too crazy, he'll stop me. He knows what you should do and shouldn't do and influences others."

Taking responsibility has earned Grant trust from his elders and peers.

"Jared, me, Clark and Grant have camped together," said

Bullins. Heading for the hills beyond Farris Park in Mayodan, the boys take a break spending a night and day in the woods. They stay up late and play games like "Capture the Flag."

As a younger brother, Clark Erskine is undaunted by his brother's continual successes.

"People say, 'That's the famous person's brother,'" says Clark. "I like it."

Now 13-years-old, Clark adds they outgrew sibling fights a few years ago.

Having his brother around scouts "makes it more fun for me."

Under no pressure to follow in Grant's footsteps, Clark is setting his own goals.

"I'm not going to the Air Force Academy," he says. "But I do plan to go for Eagle Scout."

Preferring a quieter pace, Clark wants to attend a smaller college.

Childhood antics ultimately reveal the relationship between the two older Erskine boys. Enjoying the outdoors, the boys tackled treehouses and trails.

"We built three tree houses in one day," says Clark. The first and best one fell with Clark trapped underneath.

"Grant thought I was dead," he says. But Clark was only knocked unconscious for a moment, he says. "I got up and we built two more."

Grant was allowed to host a New Year's Eve party two years ago and invited Clark.

"He always includes me," said Clark. "He treats me the same (as others) around his friends and girlfriends."

During the party, several boys played basketball outside. In a quick turn, Clark broke his nose when he hit another player.

As their parents took Clark to the hospital, Grant stayed behind with his guests.

"He worried about me at the hospital and couldn't enjoy the party," says Clark.

Exploring new experiences is a passage for teenagers going into adulthood. Unfortunately, some turn to drugs or alcohol for this ceremony. Grant turns to a positive outlet for his adventures.

"A lot of times, in your teenage years, you try new things and do something you haven't done," he says. "Service is part of that. As an American, some of us need to give back something just to make this country greater."

Although Grant blushes at the attention he receives and tries to keep a low profile, he recognizes his influence on younger children.

"You really are somebody's hero," he says. "Those little kids have faith in you and that keeps you going." 〜

# Foster Children and the "System": Is America's Promise Being Kept?

## Jennifer Kiziah

⇒⇐

A child comes to school with another black eye that he won't explain. A woman calls the Department of Social Services and says she hasn't seen her neighbor, the mother of two children, for two days. She's seen the older child helping her sister onto the school bus though, so she knows the children are at home. Could Social Services please go see what's going on?

When someone places a phone call to the police or Department of Social Services about the safety and welfare of a child, he or she sets in motion a chain of events which can lead to a child being separated from his or her biological family for several years, if not permanently. If the allegations have merit,

---

*Jennifer Kiziah, a reporter for the* Hickory Daily Record, *has covered Families for Kids and Court Improvement Project meetings during her two years at the paper. Attending the meetings has made her more aware of the importance of providing stable, loving families for foster and adoptive children and the challenges faced by those working to shorten the time-frame in which this may happen.*

children often wait in foster care while details of their lives are worked out in juvenile court.

Although the Families for Kids program advocates finding permanent homes for children within one year, many children stay in the system much longer. Catawba County was selected in October 1995 by the W.K. Kellogg Foundation to become one of eight lead sites across North Carolina to redesign the community's child welfare system. In an effort to learn more about what happens to foster children in the 25th Judicial District, representatives from the three counties in the district — Catawba, Caldwell and Burke — formed a Tri-County Child Advocacy Planning Team. The team studied cases from May 1996 to September 1997, and discovered that none of the three counties had found permanent homes for children placed in foster care within the year they were taken from their homes. Burke County averaged 2.5 years before the children were situated; Caldwell and Catawba both averaged 1.75 years. America's Promise to provide every child with an ongoing relationship with a caring adult; to provide safe places to learn and grow; and to provide a healthy start and future is not being kept if foster children must wait years before their cases are resolved.

Billie, now 17, was officially adopted a little over a year ago. She was about 11-years-old, and her brother about nine-years-old when her stepfather called Social Services to report their mother for neglect. Billie says her stepfather did not call out of any sense of concern for the children, but because of the "mind games" he and her mother liked to play. According to Billie, her mother and stepfather constantly broke up and reconciled. During one of their "off" periods, Billie says her stepfather called DSS and said their mother hadn't been around for three or four days. Soon after he made the call, a social worker and police officer arrived to take the children away. "My social worker tried to be nice," Billie says, "but when they're trying to take you away, you can't think of them except as an enemy."

Billie says her stepfather had lied, that her mother had not been gone for three or four days. She just worked second or third shift and wasn't home at certain times. Her mother's schedule, of course, meant Billie was her brother's primary caregiver. The social worker took the two children to DSS while she searched for a foster home. "I hated it there," Billie says of the foster home. "I tried to isolate myself. We were out of school for a week before they decided what to do with us."

The court allowed Billie and her brother to return to their mother with two conditions: she stay away from Billie's step-father, and that they live with Billie's aunt. It wasn't long, however, before Billie spotted her mother and stepfather in a car together — a violation of the court order. Billie told her aunt she had seen her mother and stepfather together, so her aunt threw Billie's mother out of the house. Her brother was sent to another relative. Eventually, Billie's aunt told her she was having financial problems and that she did not have room for Billie to stay with her anymore. As a result, the aunt put Billie into the Receiving Home — a temporary care facility. Although Billie said the Receiving Home is supposed to be a temporary placement, "kids end up going there and staying there two, three, four, five months at a time."

Billie says her stay at the Receiving Home was horrible and that she cried every night. The halls were rigged with alarms, so if someone had to use the restroom in the middle of the night, he or she would inevitably set off the alarm. Because the home served both boys and girls at that time, the young people were always strictly supervised. Billie hated living at the Receiving Home so much that she and another girl ran away one weekend when everyone went to a movie. At 12 years of age, Billie ran away and stayed in a hotel for two nights with her 16-year-old co-conspirator, a 17-year-old girl and several other people in their early 20's. "That was the best two days of my life," she says. "What they didn't tell me, or I probably never would have run away, is that my social worker was making arrangements for me to live with another aunt. Running away was the only way I saw out."

At that point in the process, Billie says she still felt she was simply being kept away from her mother. "She would party and call me whenever she felt like it, drunk, but I didn't care because she was my mom," Billie says. Billie lived with another aunt until she was about 13-years-old. While there, she says she took too many liberties with her freedom and ran wild. She dated a 15-year-old boy who drank alcohol, smoked marijuana, took pills and mentally abused her. They started having sexual intercourse when she was 13. Billie says she would sneak out of her aunt's house at night to meet her boyfriend, and then crawl back through her window to get ready for school the next morning.

While living with her aunt, Billie ran away one more time, after Christmas. "I felt like my aunt was griping at me all the time," Billie says. "I did things I shouldn't have done — cuss fights, popping pills. I totally had an 'I don't care' attitude." To make matters worse, when Billie ran away the second time, again with a friend, they decided to make it look like they were kidnapped. It got so out of hand that Billie's mother was notified and summoned to the morgue to identify a body. After they were caught, Billie says they lied about what had happened. She doesn't really know why she lied, but says, "I needed to get out of the house and I didn't know how to do it. And after we got caught, I didn't know how to get out of it. I totally had the defensive, shut-out-the-world attitude."

After returning to her aunt's house, Billie says she and her aunt got into a "knock-down-drag-out fight." Billie asked her social worker to remove her from the house. The social worker obliged, and Billie went back to the Receiving Home. By this time, one of Billie's friends in school knew about what had been happening. Her friend's parents agreed to take Billie into their home gradually — first on weekends, then weeknights. Eventually, the couple adopted her. "I think I've lived my life backwards," Billie says. "At 10 or 11, I was drinking, smoking cigarettes and taking care of my brother. I did everything when I was young." By comparison, her life now seems tame.

It's taken her time to understand all she's been through. In the beginning everyone acted like the court system wasn't part of her life, Billie says. It seemed a ghost that guided her life. Gradually, she became aware her life was being decided in the courtroom while she sat waiting for news. She says she had to fight to be allowed to go to court. "You're discussing my life, why shouldn't I be there?" she would ask. "Everybody else is saying, 'You don't know what you want, you don't know what's in your best interest.'"

Billie becomes critical when discussing experiences with DSS. While she says the judges were "always really nice, and they tried to be understanding," they didn't understand the whole situation. She wishes the court had been more realistic about her mother and freed her to move onto a healthier life instead of giving her mother extensive amounts of time to prove herself and to fulfill her obligations to regain custody of her children. "He [judge] told her she had six months to do this, this and this to get her kids back, and six months later we'd be back and nothing would have changed," Billie says. "She had probably four years to do maybe three months' worth of work and she never would do it. We kept going back for a six-month review and she never had done anything." Billie believes her mother should have been given one chance, or maybe two, to do what the court ordered. After that, she says, her mother's parental rights should have been terminated so Billie could get on with her life. Unlike her mother, Billie's stepfather did what the court ordered and was given custody of his son, Billie's brother.

During her adoption hearing, Billie says she liked that the judge asked her what she wanted. While she wishes judges would ask the opinion of the children more often, she says she knows what would happen if they did — the children would say they just want to go home. "I wouldn't want anyone else to go through what I did, but I was accustomed to it," Billie says. "That doesn't make it right, or the parents fit, but the child is used to it and you're trying to take them out of that and they're going to be shell-shocked, they're not going to know what to do."

When asked if she had any suggestions for improving the court system for children, she says a lot of her fear came from the intimidation she felt going into the courtroom. "Judges are just there to do their job, so I don't know what else they can do," she said. "Except, if they're having a bad day — just think of the child." As for DSS, Billie says most children may not realize the DSS attorney is not there to represent them, but to represent DSS. DSS should begin looking out for the child's welfare instead of its own, she says. "Listen to what the kids have to say," she says. "Don't tell them they don't know what they need and what they want. At least acknowledge what they're saying."

Billie also criticizes the way DSS dashes some foster kid's hopes by telling them reunification with birth parents will not happen. "Give them some other options to think about," she says. "Acknowledge and listen to their wishes, but explain that reunification may not happen." And, she says, in court someone should sit with children and explain what is happening. Overall, she says, remember the children — when they are in the system, they are somewhere they don't want to be with people they don't want to be with.

Billie says the only thing that helped her get through the court system was her Guardian ad Litem (GAL) volunteer — her advocate. The GAL is the only participant in the case whose only concern is the child. In a juvenile courtroom, a GAL volunteer makes recommendations in the child's best interests while an accompanying attorney represents the child's legal rights. Angela Phillips, GAL district administrator for Catawba, Burke and Caldwell counties, says her staff's role can sometimes conflict with other players in the courtroom. The DSS attorney represents the agency's best interest — which are not necessarily the child's. The child's parents also have their own attorneys, which are often paid for by the state. Phillips worries that the GAL program is not well-financed, and points out that the program's statewide budget to pay attorneys was cut by $505,263 in 1995, bringing the total allocation for attorneys to $900,000. She says it is ironic to hear people talk about how important children are and then watch them cut the budget of a program whose sole purpose is to represent the best interests of those children.

In the 25th Judicial District, for instance, Phillips says her program represents 524 children. Last year, the program received 187 new cases and participated in 1,656 hearings. The staff consists of 97 volunteers, four administrators and three attorneys. Those three attorneys, one for each county, received a combined $32,932 for their services in one year. According to Phillips, the state paid only $63 for each child to have a GAL attorney for the duration of his or her case.

Because of the increasing number of cases assigned to the program and its limited funds, Phillips says volunteers are sorely needed. To volunteer, a person must submit a written application, three personal/professional references and undergo a criminal record check. A GAL staff member conducts a personal interview, and those who are successfully screened must complete 20 to 30 hours of training before being sworn in by a district court judge. A GAL's duties include visiting the child; interviewing the parent, guardians or caretakers, social workers and neighbors; making the court aware of the child's wishes; preparing reports for the court; and keeping the child informed of all aspects of the court proceedings.

Phillips says if a child is 12 or older, he or she should be in the courtroom. If the children are younger, she says, it's discretionary. She prefers for the children to appear in court unless the social worker can give her a good reason why they should not. "How do they feel?" she asks, "Anxious, nervous, conflicted, but it's therapeutic for them to come to court and speak to the judge." District Court Judge Jonathan Jones says that while the wishes of younger children have very little influence on the court, the wishes of older children — ages 12, 13 or 14, for instance — can affect his decision. With young people aged 15 to 17, he said, "sometimes they know how to interfere with their placements, so everybody gives up and says, 'OK, go back to your family.'"

According to Phillips, "the majority of the children want to be with their parents no matter what, but over time, as they build trust and friendship with their guardian, they will reveal more and more of the history of the home." Phillips says children often minimize what has happened to them because they don't want to get their parents into even more trouble. One solution to the whole problem, Phillips says, would be to require all students to take a child care course by the time they enter 9th grade. Many parents who lose custody of their children had poor role models, and never learned how to take care of their own kids.

Another way to ensure that foster children receive stable, loving homes is for people to become involved in a local court improvement project. Two North Carolina judicial districts have received grants to begin court improvement projects in which juvenile courts will assess, plan and make improvements in child abuse and neglect, foster care and adoption cases. The 20th Judicial District, which consists of Anson, Stanly, Union and Richmond counties, was selected by the N.C. Administrative Office of the Courts last year to begin such a program. The 25th District, consisting of Burke, Catawba and Caldwell counties, was also chosen to participate this year. With two districts working on their own court improvement plans, officials hope their ideas will soon prove successful enough to use statewide. ☞

# Josh: A Gift
# From the Community

## Ken Brockenbrough

≈⌒

One afternoon in October 1996, a crowd of people as diverse as anyone might hope to find in Raleigh came together for a single purpose. The thread uniting this lively audience was that they had lived all or most of their lives with a disability. The mostly adult audience gathered to address several prominent state legislators and policymakers regarding the importance of technology in their lives. Whether blind, hearing impaired or dependent on wheelchairs and other devices for mobility, all came to "speak out" and advocate for better access to technologies that could improve their lives.

A young voice emerged during the audience's encounter with the panel, requesting a microphone from the back of the

---

*Ken Brockenbrough is a husband and father of three: Ben (18), Anna (16), and Marie (11). In his current role as planner for N.C. Council on Developmental Disabilities, as in past employment, he depends on his own family and the insights of other families to teach him things his Ph.D. in Child and Family Development never could.*

157

room. The audience separated politely, admitting to the front
a young man in a motorized wheelchair. He was no more than
13 or 14-years-old.

"My name is Josh Lindsey," he announced in a quiet and
jagged voice, but with absorbing confidence. "I was born with
cerebral palsy. I have had quadriplegia all my life, and I go to
a fully inclusive middle school." Undaunted by his difficulty
speaking clearly and loudly, Josh went on to describe with
the poise of an experienced speaker how his chair, computer
technology, and more importantly, the assistance of caring
adults, helped him excel as a straight A student at Durant Road
Middle School in Raleigh.

What enabled this slight young man with a bowl haircut
and broad smile to drive his chair forward and speak with such
authority to these important adults who, elevated upon the
speakers' dais, were prepared to make life-changing decisions
for people with disabilities? And who was that woman standing at the back of the room, where Josh had been waiting?
She was obviously eager to hear the impact of Josh's words.

Later I learned that Debbie Lindsey was Josh's mother. She
was the first among several caring adults, including Josh's
father, Tom, who had spotted and reinforced within Josh his
innate talents and abilities, the ones that Josh so clearly demonstrated that day. While the audience sat enraptured, it was
just another event in Josh's remarkable story.

Josh was born to Debbie and Tom Lindsey while both
were students in Gainesville, Florida in 1983. Though
Debbie did not know Josh had cerebral palsy for the first
seven to eight months of his life, she says she was prepared
in a special way for this child. Debbie was in training to
become an occupational therapist. And because of her love
for children in general, and children with disabilities in particular, she had talked with Tom during their engagement
about adopting a child with a disability. Josh was born to

them before they could pursue adoption. Because Josh did not demonstrate clear signs of any disability at the very beginning of life, Debbie was able to fall in love with Josh first and foremost as a child, no stigma attached, she says. As devout Roman Catholics, Debbie and Tom have always seen Josh as a gift, uniquely suited to their family.

Debbie decided to leave school before finishing her degree to care for Josh full time. When Josh was three-and-a-half-years-old, the Lindseys moved from Florida to North Carolina. Because the Lindseys arrived in late summer, Josh had to be placed on a lengthy waiting list for a preschool designed specifically for children with cerebral palsy. The Lindseys considered this inconvenience a blessing in disguise. Instead of waiting for an opening, they decided to enroll Josh at White Plains Children's Center, a preschool that places children with disabilities with their normally developing peers. The Lindseys have never regretted that decision.

Debbie and Tom have played separate but equally important roles in Josh's development as a fully participating member of his community. Debbie wanted to give Josh a good education, a sense of humor and a deep faith. She also wanted to make sure Josh did not fall behind other kids when he entered school. Recognizing Josh's love of language, Debbie taught him to read before he entered kindergarten. They began by playing with dried rice and beans and experimenting with a water table. They later advanced to wooden block letters. Josh learned quickly.

Tom wanted to share with Josh his love of sports and recreation. But it took Tom a little longer to adjust his dreams and expectations to Josh's physical limitations. While Josh was small, Tom would carry him outside to play with other children from the neighborhood. After Josh got his first motorized wheelchair, Tom would throw a ball to his son. As Josh grew, it became clear that he loved the games, but could best participate as an umpire. Tom would take Josh to Carolina Mudcats and Durham Bulls games. Their love of baseball drew the two even closer. Father and son even traveled to Florida to watch the Cincinnati Reds during spring training. But like most youngsters, Josh drew a small amount of independence by choosing to root for a different team than his father. He now jokes about how becoming a Braves fan gets under his Dad's skin.

Josh started Brentwood Elementary School with genuine excitement and enthusiasm. "This is the real thing!" he remembers thinking. And it seemed Josh fit in from the outset. In part that's because of special classroom aides such as Debbie Bonner. Bonner not only helped Josh in a practical sense, but also understood his need to be part of the whole classroom experience. At a time when there was no "adaptive physical education," Bonner found ways to adapt outdoor games to Josh's abilities. Looking back on his early school years, Josh recalls several adults who opened new worlds to him, enabling him to express himself and laugh at the world, including himself.

Between the third and fifth grades, Josh met several adults who understood the value of the arts and recreation in children's lives. Pierrette Sadler was a dance instructor who drew out the talents of children with physical and mental disabilities, helping them to learn dance and movement routines that she used in large recitals with other kids. Josh also recalls a chorus teacher, Mr. Sinclair, who "treated [me] like a person." He involved Josh in every school performance, placing him in the front row. Mr. Sinclair was able to look past a wheelchair and see Josh's talents. He included Josh in two talent shows. In one, Josh sang boldly with his sister, only to be rewarded with a cream pie in the face.

Another teacher, Mrs. Bernier, built upon Josh's love of the

spotlight and involved him in chorus and drama. Josh faced
a real hurdle in seventh grade when, after saving his allowance, money from school car washes and other fund raisers,
his income fell short of what he needed to participate in the
Junior Tours choral trip to Williamsburg, Va. With Mrs.
Bernier's help, the PTA made up the difference and created a
memorable experience for Josh. His finale that year came
when he took one of the lead roles in two different plays.

When Josh was 10, an aide, Wes Garner, recognized Josh's
frustration at not being able to fully participate in outdoor recreation. "Wes," Josh recalls, "believed in me." He not only
picked up on Josh's ability to officiate games, but got Josh

interested in model rocketry. Together, the two built and flew a rocket, to the delight of Josh's friends and classmates. At the end of his fifth grade year, Josh was awarded the "Spotlight on Students" award for his ability to meet obstacles and overcome them.

Not all of life's important lessons are learned in the classroom, and like other children, Josh has benefited from those lessons too. A close friend of the Lindseys asked Josh to be the godfather for their newborn girl, Brianna. There was a hitch, however: Josh had not met the church requirement that he be confirmed in the Catholic faith. While Josh had worshipped regularly with his family, he had not yet been confirmed. Brianna's parents approached the young priest who was to perform the baptismal ceremony and spoke with him about Josh, his faith and the importance he placed on personal responsibility. The priest sensed how important this was to Josh and permitted the small breach of tradition, with the understanding that Josh would continue to pursue Catholicism. It was a proud moment in Josh's life to be honored with such responsibility, and a happy one for the two families. Debbie said that it was one of many examples where Josh has inspired other parishioners to look more deeply into their own faith.

Josh Lindsey's story is replete with similar anecdotes of adults who have recognized his special gifts and enabled him to develop a sense of mission and an equally important sense of humor. Josh now attends Wake Forest-Rolesville High School. He was elected freshman vice president by his classmates. He is working in a school store with other students to raise money for an upcoming class trip to Washington, D.C.

But like most students his age, his life can go from high to low in a matter of hours. While Josh is generally unconcerned with the opinions of others, he wants his fellow teens to know that his mind is agile, even if his movements are not. Students who know Josh accept him for who he is. But some of the students, who see him only in passing in the hallways, take notice only of his wheelchair and hear his slower speech, and believe Josh has mental disabilities as well. Josh understands this stereotype and does what he can to prove otherwise.

Josh does not want his environment to have to adapt to him. He tries hard to complete his homework assignments on time, even though using a single index finger to spell out his work on a keyboard can take him hours. Josh wants desperately to fulfill his dream of becoming an attorney and serving his community, but he fears that he will not be able to keep up with the physical demands of law school. For Josh and his parents, the future seems frightening at times, as child and parents anticipate a life apart from one another. .

But Josh and the Lindseys are inspired by others who have broken barriers and succeeded. When Debbie Lindsey started a local chapter of Winners on Wheels with the help of a local Masonic Lodge, Josh had one of his first opportunities to meet an adult self-advocate, Joy Weeber. Joy, a member of the N.C. Council on Developmental Disabilities and a graduate student in N.C. State's Department of Counselor Education, has helped Josh take pride in being a person with special abilities. While Josh has lived most of his life in the mainstream, friendships with people like Joy and other children who have physical disabilities have given him a renewed sense of individuality. He has had to face the disappointment of playing recreational games with paraplegic children who also have wheelchairs, but who are better able to control their upper bodies. On the other hand, he has learned that not all children have his mental abilities and his special gifts with language.

When asked how he has become such a poised advocate, Josh says that being accepted by other kids his age has given him confidence. Joy thinks that part of Josh's exceptional maturity comes from his deep grasp of the personal realities of being an individual with a disability.

His acceptance and inclusion by friends has not only given Josh a voice to speak publicly, but also has enabled him to be at ease with himself and maintain a sense of humor. Like the younger boy who could laugh at being hit in the face with a pie, in adolescence, Josh is able to deal with situations others might find embarrassing. For instance, his classmates ask him what he does if he needs to use the bathroom at night. He is comfortable explaining his special needs to them. On the other hand, like all 15-year-old boys, Josh gets a little rattled talking about unrequited love. He has begun to ask himself how he will go on dates without being able to drive a car. One senses, however, that he will be ready to tackle that obstacle as he has most others. ⌒

# S O S:
# A Door to the Future

**D o r i s    B .    M o t t e**

≈

**66** "I feel real welcome here," Antronius (Tron) Marsh
says as he settles deeper into a chair in the "Greet-
ing Room" at East Elementary School in Monroe.
What is this lanky 5'8", 14-year-old doing in an elementary
school?

For Tron and 30 other Monroe Middle School students, East
Elementary is the home of S.O.S. (Support Our Students), an
after-school program that offers fun, friendship and adults who
care, as well as help with school work.

Tron is a friendly, well-mannered young man, eager to talk
about S.O.S. and the difference it has made in his life. Like
most of his friends in the program, he lives in Monroe, a town
of about 20,000 located 20 miles east of Charlotte.

---

*Doris Motte is a staff writer for* The Enquirer-Journal, *Monroe's local daily.
She reports on religion, education, and almost anything related to children.
In this capacity, she first met Bea Colson and became acquainted with the
S.O.S. program. Motte says she is continually impressed with the fine work
that this program does in adding stability and the hope of success to the
lives of children who might otherwise not have it.*

The state-funded S.O.S. program was introduced in 1994 by Governor Jim Hunt. Monroe's program, one of the first in the state, now involves about 150 third to eighth grade students. S.O.S.'s mission is to help prevent juvenile crime by rallying communities around their young people, and by helping to steer young people away from trouble and into positive, constructive activities. Monroe's program also adopted the concept of S.E.E.D.S. — "Specialists Educating Empowering Directing Students." For Tron and his friends, the program appears to be having the desired effect.

Like Tron, most of these middle school students have been attending S.O.S. since fourth grade. They are quick to tell you that S.O.S. is an important part of their lives. They say S.O.S. gives them something to do. It keeps them off the street and out of trouble. It helps them earn good grades.

On a beautiful spring afternoon in March, about 10 eighth grade students dressed in typical middle school garb — baggy pants, t-shirts and bright athletic shoes — stream into a classroom at East Elementary after a day at Monroe Middle School. They plop down book bags, and pull out textbooks and notebooks. They chatter and laugh together as they prepare to do their homework, the first order of every day at S.O.S.

They say if it weren't for S.O.S. they would be on the phone, asleep, playing Nintendo, or just hanging out. One lively eighth grader with a bright smile says hanging out in her neighborhood means being surrounded by drugs and "hoodrats."

Students are as enthusiastic about the academic benefits of S.O.S. as they are about the fun and friendship it provides. When asked about the benefits of the program, students invariably say it helps them make good grades, which would in turn help them in the future.

Tuesday to Thursday the focus of S.O.S. is on academics. Each day, students attend classes in three to four subjects such as math, science, social studies and computers, as well as get any tutorial help they may need.

Tron admits that social studies, which he finds boring, is where he needs the most help. But he eats up all the math and computer work he can get. He is taking Algebra I-A at Monroe Middle and plans to take as much math as he can in high school. "Math is what you really need to make it," he says.

Friday is fun day at S.O.S., with a choice of activities including recreational sports, cooking, drill team, drama, clubs, aerobics and computer games. Tron's all-time favorite activity is sports, and his first love is basketball.

Field trips are popular among students even though they must earn the right to participate. They earn points toward field trips by regular school attendance, maintaining passing grades, getting good conduct marks and turning in their homework, all of which is monitored by S.O.S. staff. They must meet the same criteria in S.O.S.

Students say the trips are well worth the effort. They have gone to Charlotte Hornets basketball games, visited Myrtle Beach, and toured Washington, D.C. and Atlanta.

Tron enjoyed the trip to Washington, D.C. the most. One week last summer, the group drove all night to get to Washington. Tron went sightseeing all day, then turned around and rode home. "Yes ma'am, we were tired and it was hot," Tron says. What did he enjoy the most? "The women," he says with a chuckle, then adds more seriously, "really, the things we got to see."

On Saturday, when your average student is sleeping late or watching cartoons on television, Tron and other S.O.S. students are at East Elementary by 7 a.m., ready to board a bus for the 45 minute drive to Johnson C. Smith University in Charlotte, where they participate in the Saturday Academy.

At JCSU they spend the day working on computers or playing sports while interacting with members of the JCSU

soccer team. They have all-you-can-eat meals in the school cafeteria.

There Tron enjoys surfing the Internet as well as being able to do more advanced work on computers than he can do at the middle school he attends. And, he never misses the opportunity to shoot a few baskets in the gym.

But the program is not just fun and games, says Bea Colson, principal of East Elementary and founder of Monroe's S.O.S. program.

"If they enjoy a college environment, they can see themselves becoming college students," Colson says. "They work with basketball and soccer teams in the computer labs and in the gym. They go into lecture halls. We help them set goals without even knowing they are setting goals. It goes back to the concept of S.E.E.D.S. — we're planting seeds."

Tron, who's 14, already has career goals in mind, and in case plan A doesn't work out, he has plan B. "I would like to go to Carolina and play basketball and eventually play in the NBA." he says. "If I don't do that, I'd like to buy out IBM."

Buy out IBM? Play in the NBA? Isn't that a bit unrealistic?

"Well, they tell us to dream big," Tron laughs. "I really like computers. If I can't get into the NBA, I'll do something with computers."

It's too early yet to say whether Tron's NBA dreams could become reality, but he is doing what he can to get ready. He plays guard on the Monroe City Recreation League basketball team. This year he made the all-star team, which went all the way to the championship round in a tournament in Winston-Salem. He hopes to hone his skills by playing basketball for Monroe High next year. He also plans to try out for baseball and football.

Tron and the other students agree that just as important as the academic help they receive and the fun they have in S.O.S. are the adults who care, who stick with them, who go the extra mile.

Colson was Tron's principal when he attended East Elementary, but their relationship goes back even farther.

"She knew me before I even started school. She's a real special person to me. Just like another mother or grandmother," he says. "I would vote for her for best principal."

"We have watched him grow," Colson says. "He is a good student. S.O.S. has helped him establish a routine. It has reaffirmed who he is, and what he needs to be. It helped him to establish goals. His mother has always said, 'you can do it.' But the program has helped him say it about himself."

Colson describes Tron's mother, Pamela Baker, as a single parent with high goals who is as active and involved in Tron's life as she is with Tron's nine-year-old sister, Peir. Baker, for her part, can't say enough about what S.O.S. has done for Tron.

"I really do believe it takes a community to raise a child," she says. "Tron has been in [S.O.S.] since fourth grade and to me it's helped him a great deal, as far as academic, social skills, personality, as far as our community is concerned. Compare him with other kids he goes to school with, and there's a considerable difference. . . . I believe he would be a different young gentleman if it wasn't for the Saturday Academy. The field trips are important, too. It's broadened his horizons."

Baker says she has always taught her children to respect their elders, but she credits S.O.S. with reinforcing her training.

"It teaches a lot more than academics," she says. "A lot of the other kids are disrespectful and downright rude. I haven't come across many kids that compare [to Tron]. He's courteous, very polite. I go to conferences with teachers at school, and everybody praises him."

Tron's mother likes that her son doesn't mind hugging her or telling her he loves her in front of his friends, even as they stand by and scoff. He faithfully participates in Friday night youth activities at the church they attend.

Tron credits S.O.S. with helping him to be a more mature teenager and make better decisions. His mother agrees.

"He's good at making decisions on his own. This year he chose not to play football for Monroe Middle because he feared it would interfere with his grades," she says. "His personality, his persona, seems older than 14."

Far from making him unpopular with his peers, Tron's personal qualities seem to attract others.

"A lot of his peers look up to him. . . . Everyone's trying to be like Tron. Everyone's got their eye on him for some reason," his mother says.

Monroe S.O.S.'s founder Colson says that for a while Tron was one of only two middle school boys in the after-school program, and because of it he has learned to be a buddy with the girls and treat them with respect. "The girls have reaffirmed who he is," Colson says. "If he wasn't here on a Saturday morning, they would call and get him out of bed and wait for him to get here."

Friendship is an important part of what S.O.S. is all about. Tron has several friends he has grown up with who are in S.O.S. "My friends, they mean a lot to me because I need them to root me on," he says.

Baker is both surprised and delighted by the way her son is maturing. "I thought by the time he was 14, it would be trouble, but he's not a rebellious child. I hope that doesn't change," she says.

When she gets discouraged in her single-parent role, she reminds herself that her mother raised seven children alone, so surely she can raise two.

"She's the rock you lean up against when you're about to fall over," Baker says of her mother, Kathy Chambers, who looked after Tron as an infant while Baker went back to school to get her training as a pharmacy technician. Later, Chambers kept Tron at night while Baker worked late shifts, and has watched him and his sister during school breaks. Now Chambers is adjusting, not entirely willingly, to the idea that Tron is old enough to be home alone when school is out.

Because many of the students in S.O.S. live in single-parent families, one of Colson's goals is to bring as many positive male role models into the program as possible. One such teacher recruited this year to direct the middle school portion of the S.O.S. program is Maurice Douglas.

"He does whatever he can to look out for you and keep you straight," Tron says. "If you need anything he'll be there. If we need to talk about anything he understands."

Although he sees his father frequently, Tron feels Douglas is an important addition to his life. "He's really my type of man," Tron says.

It was largely Colson's vision that brought S.O.S. to East Elementary, and though she is not the program director, it is clear that her energy and enthusiasm are an important ingredient in its continued success.

Colson, a Union County native, graduated from high school in 1960 at the age of 16, the salutatorian of her class. She went on to graduate *cum laude* from Johnson C. Smith University in 1964. While earning her masters degree at the University of North Carolina at Greensboro, she taught school in High Point. She then returned to Union County where she has been on the front lines of education for 30 years. She taught in three elementary schools and one middle school in the county before becoming principal of East in 1985.

Colson pauses at 5 p.m. one afternoon in March to talk about how East's S.O.S. program began. Despite the hour, the school shows no signs of closing. As after-school students leave, others pour in with parents in tow for a science and math night.

"I live like this all the time," Colson says with a laugh as she eases herself into a chair for a few moments of remembering. She recalls the marathon week she spent writing the original grant proposal for S.O.S. She learned of Governor Hunt's proposal for S.O.S. only three days before the deadline for applications. At the time, she was attending a principal's planning retreat in Boone. Undeterred by a difficult deadline, she stayed up all night writing the proposal in long hand, then faxed it to her secretary. By the time she returned to Monroe the next afternoon, the proposal was neatly typed and ready to be sent to Raleigh by overnight mail. Her efforts paid off, and the program was funded for $75,000 that first year.

Colson and the staff at East Elementary had long been working toward an extended day program that would bridge the learning gap between school and home. This was it.

"We felt the students needed it. There was so much [for children] to learn, we couldn't cram it all into one school day," Colson says. "If you look at the variation in test scores among a group of children and you realize their potential for learning is the same, there must be outside factors affecting the scores." In Colson's view, two of the factors are structure and exposure to cultural experiences, both of which she included in the S.O.S. model.

When Colson heard about S.O.S., she and her staff were ready. They had already established a mentoring program through a local business that brought black male professionals to the school to work with children. They had applied for a Z. Smith Reynolds grant suggesting a model similar to S.O.S. Though they were turned down, it helped pave the way for writing the S.O.S. proposal. A key player in the program has been Blacks Memorial Presbyterian Church, S.O.S.'s community sponsor. Last year S.O.S. opened a second site at Blacks Memorial where seven students work in a program which focuses on college prep studies.

"It goes back to the idea that planting a seed is so important. We welcome any child who is struggling. Success is what we're all about," Colson says.

Success is what it's all about for Tron and his peers as well.

"I'm trying to learn what I need to make it," Tron says.

Given the seeds that have been planted and the fruit those seeds are bearing, there seems little doubt he will. ⌐

# A Fire
# Burning Brightly

## E d   B r i s t o l

≈◦≈

RALEIGH — *A runaway car hopped a curb Wednesday and hit three Broughton High School students heading to school, injuring one critically. Police say the driver. . . who has a previous conviction for driving while impaired, appeared to be under the influence of alcohol. The injured included a brother and sister. Laura Beth Nicholson, 14, was treated and released from Wake Medical Center, but her brother Frank, 15, was in critical condition with serious head and internal injuries. Blake Schlukbier, 14, who was brushed and knocked to the ground, was not seriously injured.*

— The News & Observer, *September 26, 1996*

*Ed Bristol, a Raleigh writer, is the marketing/public relations director of Easter Seals of North Carolina and president of Bristol Associates, a public relations firm serving nonprofit and for-profit clients. He has 20 years of experience in media, advertising and public relations.*

The day of the accident, rumors and pieces of information spread quickly through Broughton High School. At first, 17-year-old Lura Forcum was incredulous that somebody would have been driving drunk at seven o'clock in the morning. But, later in the day, when the principal's office released a statement confirming the details, disbelief turned to anger.

"It's outrageous. Drinking and driving is just not something you do," Lura recalls thinking. "You don't wave around a loaded gun. You don't get in the car after you've been drinking."

"I'm not saying that high school students don't drink," she adds, "but you just don't hear about them drinking and driving that often."

Outrage over the accident galvanized the Broughton student body and would later fuel a student campaign to press for changes in the state's drunk driving laws. One of the leaders of that drive was Lura Forcum, a soft-spoken, good-natured junior with idealism, insight and conviction that she'd already put to use by volunteering at a Washington, D.C. nursery for at risk kids and on a church mission to South Korea.

"She's a doer," says Jim Forcum of his oldest child, a slim, brown-haired honors student. "Lura's never shied away from involvement, and I think people pretty quickly sense that she's purposeful and mature for her age."

Laughs her mother, Susan Forcum: "I think she was probably born mature." And determined. Susan tells about the time when Lura was seven or eight, "and she announced that her goal was to play Gershwin. Well, by her 10th grade piano recital, she was playing George Gershwin!"

Her worst fault, Lura and her parents agree, is her impatience when she feels she can't master something. But in recalling when she and other students took on the drunk driving issue, Jim and Susan say her commitment to making a difference overcame an abundance of frustration toward obstacles along the way.

In the spring following the Nicholson accident, the N.C. General Assembly began debate on a new, tougher drunk-driving bill. Among its provisions were stricter and more mandatory sentences for DWI convictions, an increase in the "automatic license revocation" period from 10 days to 30, and confiscation of vehicles owned by drivers whose licenses had been revoked as a result of a prior DWI conviction.

The old law called for mandatory sentencing for an offender's first three convictions. But with a fourth offense in a seven-year period, the law would classify the driver as a habitual offender, giving the judge more discretion in sentencing.

Ironically, the result was often that a habitual offender would be sentenced to only a few months in jail — less time than if the offender had had fewer DWI convictions.

This new measure seemed tailor-made to keep the kind of driver who had seriously injured Frank Nicholson off the road. At the time of the accident, the driver had been charged with drunk driving four times in seven years. Three of the charges had been dismissed on technicalities. Now for hitting Nicholson and two others, he was handed only a few months in jail.

The proposed bill wasn't perfect, but it was an improvement, says Karyn Brown, executive director of Mothers Against Drunk Driving (MADD) in North Carolina. Progress in the campaign against drunk driving sometimes has to come in slow, incremental steps, she adds.

"It was not the toughest law possible, but it was tough," she says. "The bill would take the discretion out of the judge's hands and take vehicles away from people who shouldn't be driving."

A member of the Principal's Advisory Council at school, Lura Forcum remembers when Principal Diane Payne mentioned the bill to the group and asked whether they thought Broughton students would be interested in expressing their support. At the time, Frank Nicholson was still recovering from the accident.

"People were watching Frank's progress closely, so our minds were definitely on that kind of thing. The principal asked us if we thought a student march in support of the bill would be something that people could handle, or would the students be offended if we took the whole school and marched for a cause like this."

The council enthusiastically endorsed the march. Later, to be safe, the principal developed special in-school activities for people who didn't want to take part. As it turned out, there were no takers. "There was a hundred percent support for the march," Lura recalls.

On April 16, 1997, within a week of the council meeting, 1,500 Broughton students, accompanied by a sprinkling of parents, reporters, the marching band, and a squadron of police vehicles, marched the 14 blocks to the state legislative building where they were joined by students from Southern Durham and Goldsboro high schools. They were greeted by Governor Jim Hunt and Lt. Governor Dennis Wicker, who thanked the marchers for their support for the bill.

Were some of the students there just to get out of going to class? Maybe, but the vast majority participated because a classmate had sustained brain damage after being hit by a drunk driver. And they didn't want it to happen again.

Still, recalls Principal Payne, "There were a lot of skeptics along the way who thought the students wouldn't take it seriously."

The skeptics were very clearly wrong, Lura says with unshakeable conviction. "The students' support for the march was the main reason it was a success."

But the mild-mannered teen's natural optimism and her faith in the legislative process would undergo some challenges in the days and weeks that followed. Opposition to the bill developed. One of the battlegrounds was a House Judiciary Committee hearing that both Brown and Lura attended. Lura remembers being amazed by the legislators' arguments against thc bill.

"I really don't see why there'd be a lot of objections to a bill like that," she says. But there were, "especially from some of the conservative proponents of 'minimal government.'

"They didn't want to see the bill passed," Lura says, her voice deepening with disbelief. "There was a lot of waffling, and the arguments were ridiculous: 'What if you have somebody who's drunk and driving a tractor? You're going to take away some family's form of livelihood.'" That argument was turned aside when somebody pointed out that, in 1989, tractors were exempted in DWI statutes.

"Then somebody asked: 'What about a woman with a drunk, abusive husband who gets the family car taken away?'" Lura dismisses that argument. "Well, the chances of that happening are not good since the judge would still have discretion in these cases."

It was "frustrating that anybody would oppose a bill like that, frustrating that we couldn't say anything, and frustrating that just the day before, thousands of their constituents had taken a one-mile walk to make their point, and they weren't responding," Lura says. "We were amazed and angry. There seemed to be a lack of things we could do to encourage others to vote for the bill."

Lura's discouragement lessened when DWI victim Frank Nicholson, one of the students attending that the hearing, thanked his classmates for what they were doing. Lura hadn't known Frank before his accident. Now they were joined in common cause.

Karyn Brown is still surprised that anybody could oppose the bill. "There were people who would throw things out just so there couldn't be a vote that day. I think they just wanted to kill the bill."

But the bill wasn't dead yet. Brown went to work and provided lists of legislators opposed to the bill to Lura and a handful of other volunteers. Lura remembers that one of the bill's opponents had written to Broughton honors students after report cards had come out, congratulating them on their academic achievement, and asking "us to contact him if he could ever assist us. I thought, actually, he could do something, so I gave him a call." (He wound up voting for the bill.)

Lura typed up legislators' phone numbers and a summary of the bill and set about trying to get her classmates and others to call their representatives. That effort became part of a united front committed to a tougher DWI law — and it paid off. After a conference committee ironed out differences between House and Senate versions, the bill was passed.

A few days later at a special ceremony, Lura Forcum and Karyn Brown watched as Governor Hunt signed the bill into law.

Looking back on Lura's work on the bill, Brown says "there were a couple of days when Lura didn't think the bill was going to get passed" and recalls her "passion in wanting to get the bill passed and knowing, at such a young age, how important it was.

"It's so easy when you're at that age to be swayed by the rest of the group. She has very set ideas about certain issues and she has the backing to support her ideas. A lot of young people have opinions but often don't know why they have those opinions. Lura is just far beyond her years in that regard."

After the DWI bill passed, Brown realized she might be able to make further use of Lura's passion in the day-to-day work of MADD's state headquarters in Raleigh.

Lura had been thinking about getting involved in something like MADD when Brown called her about coming to the bill signing. As they talked, Lura asked her about intern opportunities.

They sealed the deal, Brown recalls, even though "we had

never had anybody younger than college-age to inquire about coming to work at the state office."

The mission of Mothers Against Drunk Driving is "to stop drunk driving and support the victims of this violent crime," Brown says. To achieve the first objective, MADD staff work to increase public awareness and pass legislation.

Achieving the second objective is more complicated, says Brown. "For victims, the legal process is very difficult to understand at any time. I can't even imagine trying to understand it at the same time I'm grieving the loss of a loved one or recovering from some severe injuries caused by a drunk driver.

"We're able to provide that victim with assistance and also help them in the grieving process to understand what is normal, what isn't normal, and what other services are available to them. These are things that people wouldn't normally know."

Although 30 North Carolina counties now have "victim advocates" to assist survivors, the overall task is still daunting. The MADD staff couldn't manage it without the help of volunteers and interns, including the state MADD office's youngest ever.

"Lura has given to MADD so much of her time and her effort," says Brown. "It's been a wonderful experience for our older students and for us. Lura's an extremely bright individual and has the ability to apply her own critical thinking skills, form judgments on her own, and initiate movement on her own. She's not like most students her age who wait to be told what to do."

Another quality seems especially cut out for her work at MADD. "She just has care and compassion," Brown says. "You can see it in her face and hear it in her voice."

Brown laughs that an older college intern once looked at Lura's work and remarked, "she writes better than I do!" But, she adds, "they just love her and can't believe somebody her age is doing what she's doing. She does phenomenal work and we think the world of her. She's just a very special person."

Nationally, MADD has endorsed legislation to lower the legal blood alcohol content of drivers to below .08 percent. (North Carolina is one of only a handful of states to have already passed such legislation.) Lura is writing letters to senators and representatives in other states encouraging the lower limit.

Brown also plans to put Lura's legislative experience to work on other tasks — organizing support for a measure requiring registration of keg buyers to discourage supplying beer to underage drinkers and for a separate bill that closes a loophole punishing 19 or 20-year-olds less severely for possessing beer than possessing wine or liquor.

"Aside from education, the only thing you can do about drunk driving is discourage people from doing it through harsher penalities," she says, "and I think [the system] is doing the best it can."

"I have a lot of confidence in the political system," Lura says. "I think it is a wonderful process. If it wasn't, it wouldn't have lasted as long as it has. Where it has 'failed' is a result of people not knowing how to use it. I don't think everybody knows how to get in touch with their legislator or how to get an idea into a bill."

In the case of the tougher DWI bill, the system worked far better as a result of people like Lura Forcum, who helped organize the springtime march. In December, a few days after passage of the bill, Lt. Governor Wicker paid a visit to Broughton High School and told his audience: "I cannot tell you the number of legislators who came up to me and said how effective the students were."

And for her part, working for tougher DWI measures and spending after-school hours doing the "grunt" work nec-

essary to spread the MADD message, Lura received special recognition.

A MADD news release, issued December 4, 1997, tells the story:

"Lura Forcum, a student at Broughton High School, is the 1997 recipient of the Jay Bright Award for Drunk and Drugged Driving Prevention. Sponsored by Mothers Against Drunk Driving and the Governor's Highway Safety Program, the award is given to a young person under 21 who has effectively promoted the dangers of DWI."

[The award is named in honor of a 17-year-old Greenville youth, John Dorenus Bright, who in 1981 was struck from behind and killed by a drunk driver as he attempted to push his stalled automobile off the highway. His mother, Katherine Prescott, would later serve as the national president of MADD.]

"Lura has seen the DWI issue up close," the release continued. "It was the serious injury to a fellow student that rallied an entire school. One of the students who took an active role in rallying the students has been a fixture in the MADD state office, volunteering her time and making a difference in this community and state. Lura Forcum represents the good in young people today. . . ."

Of the award, Lura says, "I wasn't expecting to get that at all. It was quite an honor." Then she adds, smiling shyly, "I didn't do anything out of the ordinary. I was just trying to pitch in." ⌐

# Promises to Keep . . .
# And Miles To Go
# Before We Sleep

## Jonathan P. Sher

∽◠

I wanted to know more. About important parts of the picture that couldn't be captured within these snapshots. About why the harm done to some of these children was neither prevented, nor effectively remedied much earlier. About how to inspire in others the courage and compassion, the power and perseverance that shines forth from these portraits of young North Carolinians and the adults who shape their lives. About what will happen next to each of them.

Wanting to know more is a tribute to everyone involved in *Keeping America's Promise to North Carolina's Children*. All these stories held my interest. Some engaged my mind by provoking a host of questions, while others captured my heart.

*Dr. Jonathan P. Sher is President of the North Carolina Child Advocacy Institute. He also serves as a Vice-Chair of the Covenant with North Carolina's Children (a broad coalition of statewide and state-level organizations working together to advance public policy that benefits all of North Carolina's children and youth).*

This collection of stories never was intended to be a compre-
hcnsive overview of North Carolina's children and youth.
Other publications, such as the NC Child Advocacy Institute's
*Data Guide to Child Well-Being*, offer the global, quantitative
perspective. Instead, this book presents a more individualized,
intimate and illustrative sample of young North Carolinians,
and of the adults across our state who strive to help them.

So, what does this "illustrative sample" actually illustrate?
While there are many good answers to this question, three
have stuck with me over time. **First, this collection of true
stories illustrates the enormous diversity among North
Carolina's young people**. From Chapter 1 in which Myra
emerges from a dark closet at the age of four and blossoms
in the light of her foster/adoptive family's love, through Chapter 22 in which high school student Lura Forcum's advocacy
against drunk driving helps create a silver lining around the
dark cloud of preventable teen injuries and deaths, it becomes
increasingly obvious that the whole idea of an "average" or
"typical" North Carolina child (or childhood) is a myth.

Even this sampler only scratches the surface of North
Carolina's diversity. Growing up on Ocracoke Island can be
very different from growing up in one of Charlotte's Latino
mini-barrios. Although separated by a mere two hour drive, a
child being raised in a poor black family within rural
Northampton County may have little in common with a child
being raised by a black professional couple in suburban Wake
County. Adolescence for a Native American youth in Chero-
kee may feel and be remarkably unlike adolescence for the
child of white academics living in Chapel Hill.

The big dividing lines in American society (wealth, race,
education, religion, geography, language/culture) cut across
North Carolina, too — and they dramatically impact the lives
of children, and the nature of childhood, throughout our state.
These narratives remind us it is *not* a coincidence that

America's Promise comes closest to be being met, and will be easiest to sustain, in well-educated, upper middle class, suburban communities. They also challenge us to change this particular *status quo* . . . and to hold firm in the faith that America's Promise *can* be kept to *all* our kids.

Nevertheless, the young people we see throughout the pages of this book silently beseech us not to be so focused on these big dividing lines that we lose sight of the daily realities that loom very large in their lives. Of course, race, wealth and other such differences matter a great deal. But, so do other, more personal factors. These stories are a plea to take seriously both the general and the particular forces that influence the fate of these young North Carolinians.

Indeed, one of the great strengths of *Keeping America's Promise to North Carolina's Children* is that its stories cannot be pigeon-holed as tidy little lessons in sociology. The big dividing lines described so far can be seen in each chapter, but they mainly set the scene for the stories themselves. Again and again, the chapters rivet our attention on the power and pervasiveness of another kind of diversity — that of family and individual differences. In fact, *seen through the eyes of young North Carolinians*, the big dividing lines in our society may seem less immediately important than the more personal ones that define their daily experiences.

The 22 true tales of growing up in our state today remind us that whether a child is raised by a strong, competent, loving family dedicated to that child's success matters at least as much as whether that child's community context is urban or rural, working class or wealthy, white or of color. At the same time, these narratives implicitly urge us to see and treat each child as an *individual*, not merely as a representative of a larger group.

The gifts and challenges with which each child is endowed at birth are unique — as are the ways in which each child's nature is supported (or thwarted) by that child's environment. Honoring and respecting each child's individual diversity is an essential part of healthy child development and an irreplaceable stepping stone toward a healthy society.

The adults featured in these stories — while a very diverse group in their own right — share the common attribute of understanding and building upon the uniqueness of the child or children they help. Their success may be due, at least in part, to their ability to see each child whole and to treat each child holistically.

**Second, this anthology illustrates the complexity of life among North Carolina's children and youth today**. Even if we know better, many of us like to hang onto the idyllic image of childhood as a fairly uncomplicated and sheltered time of preparation for adulthood. Even the slogan that "our children are our future" carries within it the idea that their significance is in what they will *become*, rather than who they are right now. It also suggests their *real* lives will begin once they have grown up.

Yet, what leaps off the pages of these stories is a sense of how very real, complicated and immersed in the adult world the lives of these young North Carolinians are already. Aldin and Aldina Kulovac are war refugees who have experienced "adult" life at one of its cruelest extremes. Josh Lindsey's ability not only to cope with cerebral palsy every day of his 15 years, but also to construct an engaged and engaging personality is a heroic effort to make the most of his real life in the here and now. Thirteen-year-old Aubyn Burnside has negotiated successfully in the adult world to create her "Suitcases for Kids" program that helps to ease the all-too-real burdens of foster children. Like so many other children featured in this collection, these young North Carolinians are far removed from the kind of blissfully innocent childhood exemplified by TV's Opie Taylor in Mayberry, NC only a generation ago.

The coming generation needs and deserves the assistance of all able adults to help improve the quality of life for youths in the present and to better prepare them to succeed in the future. The 22 portraits in this anthology yield some lessons about the kinds of adult help that truly are helpful to North Carolina's children and youth. The adult heroes celebrated here share some common characteristics:

- an ability to listen, to empathize and to respect the children and youth with whom they are interacting — without abdicating their responsibility to be, and act as, the *adults* in these stories;

- a willingness to make personal, occupational and material sacrifices in support of the kids to whom they have made a commitment — i.e., placing the needs of the children ahead of their own wants; and,

- a capacity for perseverance over time and through adversity — i.e., a stubborn determination to enhance the well-being of children against the odds.

**Third, this cross-section of examples illustrates the wisdom, power and connectedness of the five Promises we all should make, and keep, in relation to every young North Carolinian**. Every chapter in this volume speaks directly at least to one Promise and most of the stories encompass multiple, inter-related Promises. The America's Promise movement deserves to be more than a passing fad. The five Promises:

1) An ongoing relationship with a caring adult
2) Safe places and structured activities during non-school hours to learn and grow
3) A healthy start and a healthy future
4) A marketable skill through effective education
5) An opportunity to give back through community service

are as crucial to the well-being of our children and youth as they are straightforward and easy to understand.

We are an embarrassingly long way from actually meeting all these Promises to all young North Carolinians. *However, the fundamental message of this movement — and of this book — is that these Promises can and must be kept.*

There are serious obstacles along the path toward turning these five Promises into effective action. Ironically, the same "systems" (e.g., education, child welfare, health, mental health and juvenile justice) are simultaneously part of the problem and part of the solution. The good news is that there are so many capable and caring individuals who work within each of these child-related systems across our state. The bad news is that these systems have taken on a life of their own — and unfortunately, it is a life that too frequently is disconnected from, and unresponsive to, the real needs, aspirations and potential of the young North Carolinians they are supposed to serve. Changing these big systems for the better is possible and necessary, but neither quick nor easy.

Perhaps the best news is that our state's children and youth do not have to wait for these massive systems to be transformed in order for their lives to improve significantly. The key to making a difference in the here and now is for our adults to give priority to the first of the five Promises: i.e., that *every young North Carolinian will have an ongoing relationship with a caring (and competent) adult.* From my perspective as a child advocate and as a parent, this Promise ranks as the first among equals. The stories in this book collectively affirm that the absence of such a relationship lies at the core of kids' problems — and that the presence of such a relationship often is the gateway to lasting improvements in children's lives.

In previous generations, it was presumed this relationship *would* exist (except in very unusual instances) between children and their birth parents. The assumption was that parents would serve as each child's advocate in dealing with the systems affecting them. Parents also were expected to act as the caring, competent adults who would guide young people in making sense of the complexities of the world around them and then, in learning how to make wise choices among the options available to them.

What has *not* changed over time is the profound need of every child and youth to be guided, nurtured, loved and disciplined by a caring, competent adult who is consistently and deeply involved in their lives — i.e., by someone who sees them whole, treats them holistically and is heavily invested in their upbringing.

What *has* changed is that an ever increasing number (perhaps even approaching a majority!) of young people across North Carolina and from all walks of life do not have such a relationship with even one adult . . . including one of their own birth parents. These children already are paying dearly for this loss. So will the rest of us . . . and sooner rather than later.

The irony is that today's young people have more interactions with more adults outside their family than any previous generation. However, these contacts with adults tend to be narrow in scope, fragmented and/or sporadic. For example, the same child may be viewed and treated as:

- a student who must pass certain tests;
- a patient to be treated;
- a case to be managed;
- a consumer to be targeted;
- a player to fill a particular role on a team; and
- a soul to be saved.

None of these are inherently bad ways for adults to think about, and interact with, children and youth. Indeed, all of these adult contacts could have positive consequences for this child. Nevertheless, without at least one adult who acts on the knowledge that this is first and foremost a child to be raised with love and good guidance, another young life will be deeply diminished. No amount of professional service can replace every child's profound and enduring need to be parented.

While there still are a significant number of North Carolina's children and youth whose access to necessary services is woefully inadequate, there also is a growing segment of young North Carolinians who are being *over-serviced and under-parented*. Both groups have a very hard row to hoe. Improving access to services is something we know how to do. Our failure to do so is a reflection of our collective lack of will and compassion, rather than any lack of know-how. By contrast, we have not yet figured out how best to prevent or remedy the wholesale abdication of parental responsibility and involvement that plagues our kids.

We also have failed to effectively change society's refusal to back up its pro-family rhetoric with the resources, education, assistance and support parents and families need to succeed. There are major steps we should take here in North Carolina to help birth parents fulfill their responsibilities to the children they have created. These range from home visitation and family preservation programs to genuinely family-friendly workplaces. We also need to find new and innovative ways of providing every child lacking an effective birth parent with the adult guidance and nurture they must have to thrive. The America's Promise movement has the potential to help on both fronts.

While I give top priority to the first of America's Promises, it is clear that all five of them are urgently important to the future of our state's children and youth. Achieving the other four Promises in NC will depend largely on the proper balance of power, resources and responsibilities among the public sector (government at all levels), the private sector (businesses), the independent sector (nonprofit organizations, including faith-based groups) and interested individuals throughout North Carolina.

We're getting better at building and sustaining effective partnerships among these groups, but much work remains. The Promises to young North Carolinians cannot be kept by any one of these groups acting alone. They only can be accomplished by working well together.

There is ample reason for optimism. North Carolina is blessed with an abundance of dedicated, competent leaders in all these sectors. We also are blessed with many "ordinary" youth and adults — such as those profiled here — in every corner of our state who have demonstrated their capacity and commitment to accomplish extraordinary things. The next step is to expand this core group and create a critical mass of our state's adults who are ready, willing and able to take one or more of these five Promises to heart — and then to transform their good intentions into meaningful action. If you have not done so already, you, too, can become a part of — and a partner in — *Keeping America's Promise to North Carolina's Children.*

My first reaction to these 22 true stories was to want to know more. Over time, my response increasingly has been to want to do more. Our fellow citizens portrayed here — young and old, able-bodied and physically handicapped, urban and rural, white and of color, rich and poor — already are making a positive difference. Now it's our turn to show how much we can do. Together, we can make North Carolina a better place in which to **be** a child and to **raise** a child. Together, we can ensure that all five of America's Promises are made, kept and never broken. Together, we can! ⟶

# Resources

## North Carolina Child Advocacy Institute (NCCAI)

311 East Edenton Street
Raleigh, NC 27601-1017
919-834-6623
www.ncchild.org

In existence since 1983, NCCAI is the only statewide, independent, non-partisan, multi-issue organization working to improve the well-being of all NC children and youth below the age of eighteen. NCCAI pursues three inter-related areas of activity: public action, public policy and public information. Through public action, NCCAI trains and leads groups and individuals to act on behalf of children. In the public policy arena, the Institute makes certain that the best interests of children and youth are represented when decisions that impact them are made. In 1995, the Institute helped create the Covenant with North Carolina's Children, a coalition of more than 85 statewide organizations advancing public policy to benefit children in NC. Known as North Carolina's most reliable and respected independent source of information on children, NCCAI launched the *Knowledge Exchange* in 1997. The *Knowledge Exchange,* an information and referral resource providing accurate, up-to-date facts and figures about children and youth, is easily accessible through our world wide website (www.ncchild.org).

**Covenant with North Carolina's Children**
PO Box 28268
Raleigh, NC 27611
919-846-1432
www.ncchild.org/98cov.htm

**Communities in Schools of North Carolina**
222 North Person Street
Raleigh, NC 27601
800-849-8881
919-832-2700
www.cisnc.org

Communities in Schools of North Carolina (CISNC) is part of the nation's largest stay-in-school network. CISNC assists communities in replicating the CIS program and provides ongoing training and technical assistance, builds statewide partnerships, serves as a statewide resource center and advocates for children, youth and their families. CISNC operates in 28 counties with plans to expand to 17 more. Local CIS programs serve more than 25,000 students at almost 200 sites. CIS is a partner of America's Promise; Governor Jim Hunt appointed Communities in Schools of North Carolina the official America's Promise liaison for North Carolina.

**America's Promise — The Alliance for Youth**
909 North Washington Street, Suite 400
Alexandria, VA 22314
800-365-0153
703-684-4500
www.americaspromise.org

America's Promise—The Alliance for Youth is a national not-for-profit organization dedicated to improving the lives of our nation's more than 15 million youth at risk. Founded in Philadelphia, PA., at the Presidents' Summit for America's Future, America's Promise aims to provide every at risk child in America with access to the fundamental resources needed in order for them to lead happy, healthy and productive lives.

*Information on how to become
a foster and/or adoptive parent*
CARE-LINE Information and Referral Service
Office of Citizen Services/NC Department of Health
   & Human Services
800-662-7030 or 919-733-4261

*Learn how to advocate for children in foster care*
Guardian ad Litem (GAL) volunteer hotline
800-982-4041

*Information packets/service project to benefit children in
foster care created by Aubyn Burnside*
Suitcases for Kids
PO Box 669
Newton, NC 28658

***Christy Sanderson's service project for
children in distressed situations***
Operation Toybox
114 White's Lane
Louisburg, NC 27549
919-554-1410
e-mail: optoybox@mindspring.com
web address: www.redcross.org./triangle/toybox

***Statewide information resource for
parents of children with disabilities***
Family Support Network
800-852-0042

***Arthur West's community based alternative
program for teens***
Operation HOPE
PO Box 25067
Durham, NC 27701

***Academic enrichment and recreational activities
for school-age kids***
Governor's Office of Citizen & Community Services
  —Volunteer Connection
Support Our Students (SOS)
877-SERVE NC

***Information on adolescent pregnancy prevention
and teen parenting***
Adolescent Parenting Program
CARE-LINE
Office of Citizen Services/NC Department of Health
  & Human Services
800-662-7030 or 919-733-4261

***Finding good quality child care***
NC Child Care Resource & Referral Network
800-CHOOSE-1

***Information on graduated drivers license***
Kay Windsor
8900 Harpers Grove Lane
Clemmons, NC 27012

Rob Foss, Ph.D.
UNC Highway Safety Research Center
730 Airport Road
CB #3430
Chapel Hill, NC 27599-3430
919-962-8702

Portia McLean
NC Department of Transportation
Research and Development
PO Box 25201
Raleigh, NC 27611
919-733-9770

***Combat abuse and neglect in NC; promote positive discipline***
Prevent Child Abuse NC
800-354-KIDS

***Join the campaign against alcohol-impaired drivers***
Mothers Against Drunk Driving (MADD)–NC
800-248-6233

# *Photo Credits*

*Wheels of Steel* — Jeff Smith

*Seeing Them Smile* — Chad Pulley

*Unconventional School Unlocks Learning* — Kent D. Johnson
(reprinted with permission from The Charlotte Observer)

*Suitcases for Kids* — Linda Burnside

*Larry's Kids* — Cash  Michaels

*De-Jing Finds Himself Again in America* — Ralf Thiede

*Hope, Love, Charity... and Basketball* — Paul Bonner

*S O S:  A Door to the Future* — Doris Motte

*A Fire Burning Brightly* — MADD-NC